A Double Minded Man

The Story of A Secret Service Agent

By Glenn Wilson

A Double Minded Man

No part of this book may be reproduced or transmitted in any form or means, electronic or mechanical, including photocopying, recording or by any information storage and retrieval systems, without written permission from the author.

Submit requests to adoublemindedman@gmail.com

Copyright © 2016 Glenn Wilson
All rights reserved.
ISBN-13: 978-1537724171
ISBN-10: 1537724177

DEDICATION

To my wife for life and best friend Mic
and to my fabulous children Tessa and Dustin
Charles and Marchelle
Who continue to believe in me and have joined
the fight to set the captives free!

A Double Minded Man

CONTENTS

Chapter		Page
	Dedication	iii
	A Double Minded Man	vii
	Introduction	ix
	Authors Note	xii
1	One For One	1
2	The Early Years	11
3	Job Change	21
4	State Police	27
5	My Family	33
6	Basics	41
7	Training	49
8	The Padded Room	57
9	Ruben	63
10	Boris	67
11	The Doberman	77
12	SFO Ford	85
13	Kennedy	91
14	The Reverend	97
15	New Orders	105
16	C.A.T.	113

CONTENTS

Chapter		Page
17	Surgery/Recovery	123
18	Life is Cheap	133
19	NSS	141
20	The Newsy	151
21	Threat from Winnemucca	157
22	Carol - The Office Manager	167
23	Former President Ford	173
24	Nicknames	179
25	Long Beach	183
26	The Old Pueblo	195
27	Falsely Accused	205
28	Los Angeles Again	221
29	The Russians	225
30	Payback	247
31	Exiting	257
32	NSS Again	273
33	Only The Best	279
	Conclusion	283
	Author's Note	285
	Disclaimer	287

A Double Minded Man

A DOUBLE MINDED MAN IS UNSTABLE IN ALL HIS WAYS
James 1:8

This is the story of one man's 20 year journey through the shadowy world of the US Secret Service. A position that not only requires you to look after the well being of the most powerful person on the planet, but also change hats and work covertly safeguarding the financial integrity of the US monetary system.

This is a story of transformation, how a naive young man, who saw things in black or white, right or wrong, survived in a world of gray.

A world that had been left behind until the September 11, 2001 terrorist attacks carried out by 19 individuals changed the American way of life forever.

The new world required a new response. A new justice and retribution. It required a very specific set of skills - skills that had to be executed with deadly accuracy.

Ex Secret Service Agent Wilson possessed those skills.

A Double Minded Man

INTRODUCTION

I noticed that every time I take a life, part of me also dies. Maybe it's part of my soul, my spirit or part of my humanity. Or maybe it's all my imagination.

I grew up in a lower middle-class family with four kids to feed on a janitor's salary. Needless to say, we ate lots of beans, bologna, Velveeta cheese and saltine crackers. If things were good, we had casseroles, Hamburger Helper and spaghetti. On the not so good days, dinner would consist of a glass of milk and a section of cornbread to crumble into your milk. My brother and I supplemented our family's protein intake by hunting and fishing.

Generally, I felt nothing when I killed a rodent, bird or reptile. But anything larger than a dog always bothered me. I think it was mostly watching the dying process. The twitching, the eyes looking at you, the panting and worst of all, the exhalation of breath as life leaves the animal's body once and for all time.

It's much easier to squeeze the trigger of a rifle at a living person a few hundred yards away and know they are dead without having to watch the whole dying process. From a distance, even with a scope, you don't see the shock, the twitching, or the fear in their eyes. You don't hear their final breath leave their lungs. Most of all, you don't watch their soul leave their bodies. Without those images embedded in your subconscious, a man can still sleep at night.

Killing is not a noble or courageous thing. But, a life fought for others can be noble and courageous, maybe even a righteous thing.

I prefer not dying for my country or its citizens, but I also have no problem helping enemies of America who are willing to die for their cause or their country.

Introduction

Author's Note

Agent's and suspects names have been changed to protect their identity. Any resemblances or similarities to actual Agent personnel, or suspects or other individuals is unintended.

A Double Minded Man

A Double Minded Man

-1-

ONE FOR ONE

Lying in the exhaust vent, who would suspect? Never be where someone would expect you to be. That's a rule I live by. After that shot --they wouldn't even know which direction to look. Making the shot is the easy part. The hard part is getting away afterwards.

I believe the liberal, politically correct ideology of today has undermined our military, raised our taxes, destroyed our healthcare and created the greatest debtor nation in the history of the world. Some worthless politicians have no regard for the Constitution of the United States or the Judeo-Christian free enterprise principles this country was founded on. In fact, they are even rewriting our history books to leave out those principles.

A Double Minded Man

These so-called public officials are only concerned about their own power. They exempt themselves and their staff from the very laws with which they burden society.

Have Americans really become so stupid that they elect these people to govern them? Or has the system of free elections become so corrupt that they are able to elect themselves?

Every time a person is slain with a fire arm, these liberal "servants of the people" want to abolish the second amendment right for citizens to own guns. Guns don't kill people! People kill people! Before there were guns, people killed each other with swords and spears and rocks. Maybe we should blame forks for making two thirds of Americans fat and pass laws to abolish the ownership and use of eating utensils.

So many of our elected officials rapidly forget the meaning of the term "public servant." You no longer even hear that term. Politicians now believe they are entitled to more than the citizens who elected them and pay their salaries and provide them with their extravagant benefits. Most believe the public exists to serve the elected. How much more of this hypocrisy will Americans take? Most Americans I know just want to feel safe and be left alone to conduct

One For One

their business and live their lives and enjoy their families. But to feel safe bad people need to be eliminated, not tolerated.

I don't play God. Others make those decisions. I and people like me simply carry out the execution. Thus, the world is a better, safer place because of things that go on behind the scenes, allowing Americans and other citizens the freedom to go to their jobs and live their lives. They can talk on their smart phones, watch their giant flat screen TVs, waste countless hours staring at computer screens and take their kids to soccer games on Saturday.

I am not cynical. Just a realist who believes most people don't have a clue that there are dark evil forces that must constantly be kept in check or the life they enjoy will disappear.

Unfortunately, we now live in a dumbed down country whose citizens don't know their history and elect leadership that want to be accepted by their enemies, rather than feared. We were a great nation when we were feared. That's what keeps a country safe. If you are big and strong, who is going to attack or provoke you into a fight knowing it will end in their destruction? Big strong guys are rarely involved in fights. People don't mess with them.

A Double Minded Man

Unless we are genetically reengineered, war and violence is a human enterprise that will always be with us. Human nature is a constant. To think that evil, power hungry people can be reasoned with is a foolish endeavor. The only thing that has changed through human history is the delivery systems of violence and who is delivering it.

Our enemies, because of their strategic geographical locations and large quantities of mineral resources that Western societies demand, now have access to unearned knowledge and excessive wealth.

The United States has limited its ability to successfully win a conflict because of rules and regulations they have placed upon themselves that nobody else abides by. Rules established by spineless, overpaid, corrupt politicians who have never even been in a school playground scuffle, let alone worn a military uniform.

War is war. Fights are fights. The rule should be: do whatever it takes to win. We are dealing with enemies who only want Americans dead. Our enemies don't want to get along or convert you to their way of thinking or religion. They only want you dead. Americans need to pull their head out and realize they are not entitled to life, liberty and the pursuit of happiness. Those rights are only available to them if they are willing to fight for them. If Americans don't soon realize this, they will eventually be living in bondage.

We are dealing with enemies who have no rules, regulations or limitations placed upon their violent capabilities. Enemies that hate everything about us. Who we are, our culture and what we do and they only want to annihilate us. Instead of making our citizens aware of this, we now live in a society where we have US leaders and officials apologizing for America's successes of the past and providing aid and weapons to countries who want to destroy America. How can American leadership think that is what's best for it citizens?

They believe that if we reduce our capabilities of wealth and power, then we will become acceptable to our enemies and they will no longer feel threatened by the United States. We can then all hold hands and sing "We Are The World", and put "coexist" stickers on our cars. How naïve! When the unseen, unknown defenders of our way of life are no more, we will also be no more.

We are dealing with theocratic zealots who are anxious to die and receive their eternal re-

A Double Minded Man

ward. We must be vigilant and assist them in their efforts. Maybe misguided Americans feel that they are in no danger from our nation's enemies. They believe that if something should happen that our military will suddenly rally and defend their way of life.

It's all too easy for some Americans to sit in their lazy boy recliners eating pizza, drinking beer, watching and screaming for their favorite sports team and tolerate our biased liberal media criticizing our brave American military abroad. They are on foreign soil defending American's ability to engage in those worthless activities.

So here I am: lying in the dark, dirty, confined ducting, five feet from the exterior opening of the fresh air vent. Hidden from sight, I have the crosshairs of my Leopold scope on the head of a man with a name I can't pronounce; whatever. It matters not to me. It's only a target that I need to strike. I clear my mind, become one with the weapon. Nothing else matters. I am gently applying pressure with my right forefinger to the cold hard steel of the specially modified M4 rifle.

As I gently exhale, I increase the trigger pressure. Suddenly, without warning the hammer strikes hitting the center fire cartridge and the specially designed Alloy bullet is on its way to its target. So intense was my focus that I am not even aware of the rifles recoil against my right shoulder or the silenced muzzle blast.

Instantly, I see the impact occur. The reddish gray splatter as the targets head explodes in a combination of blood, brain, bone and hair. A sight, I had witnessed many times before. At 300 yards, this was an easy shot compared to cantaloupes at 1200 yards; now that's a challenge!

Yet, the target was not a victim, but a terrorist. A theocratic zealot, who was in the process of triggering an explosive dirty bomb that would have killed, wounded and disfigured scores of innocent Americans - fathers, mothers, grandparents and children. Uncaring for the grieving ripple effect the deaths and injuries will have on countless friends, relatives, associates, coworkers and others whose lives are interwoven with the dead and injured.

These terrorists could care less. Their only goal is to destroy Americans and spread terror and fear. They hate us and all we represent to them. They cannot and do not want to change or get along. Like a cancerous tumor, they must be removed.

This action and all traces of it must be destroyed. No report or official record of this incident will ever be made.

The liberal enlightened thinkers of our society would never agree with such actions. They have no comprehension of the evil that surrounds them, that if left unchecked will gladly and willingly destroy them and all they represent and care about.

But my task is not to think philosophically or justify such actions. Mine is but to execute, terminate and carry out the order.

See how simple that is. It's good versus evil. Right versus wrong. Problem solved. Next.

Now I can go home to the wife and kids. Ask about their day. Lie to them about mine. Listen to the children say their prayers. Go to bed and pretend everything is right with the world.

I am a divided, conflicted man. Two people in one body. One a quiet, conservative family man. One a deadly, violent executioner.

One For One

A Double Minded Man

-2-

THE EARLY YEARS

I grew up in Oroville, California. It was a small town of about 9,000 in the foothills of Butte County, about 80 miles north of Sacramento. Oroville got its name from the Gold Rush days of California when the "49ers" discovered gold at Sutter's Mill in 1849 and thus began the California Gold Rush. Soon all of Northern California was full of gold miners hoping to strike it rich. Oroville and the surrounding area are still covered with the geographical scars of the Gold Rush.

Chinese immigrants were brought in to construct a great rock wall that completely diverted the Feather River, which bisected the town of Oroville; this allowed the miners to extract gold from the dry riverbed.

The surrounding hills are full of mining tunnels, but most have been blocked off to keep the curious from exploring these dangerous passageways.

Large floating mechanical barges called dredgers floated in the waterways of the Feather River and scooped up tons of riverbed. The material was then run through screens in search of gold. The leftover rock, gravel and earth covered the riverbank for miles and remained that way for over a century.

These remains and the derelict equipment were my playground as a child. Exploring abandoned mine shafts, playing on abandoned gold dredges and exploring miles of man-made mountains of rock and earth created by the dredging made for an active childhood.

After the gold rush, the area's economy consisted of logging and lumber mills. The Western Union railroad also had a large presence as a result of the lumber industry. Louisiana Pacific also operated a creosote plant, which is a black petroleum based chemical applied to railroad ties and utility poles as a preservative.

Depending upon the direction of the wind, you could smell the creosote for miles.

The Early Years

The best job to be had in the town of Oroville was a position at the RCBS plant. The company made ammunition reloading equipment for the world. All RCBS employees were mainly assembly line workers, but the pay was good and so were the benefits. However, you had to know someone on the inside if you hoped to get hired. Many of my friends who graduated from Oroville High School obtained jobs in the lumber mills, the railroad or RCBS and never left the area.

The 20th century economic boom for Oroville occurred in the 1960s, when the California Department of Water Resources decided to build a dam across the Feather River. This was a monumental task and created several thousand jobs and brought many new families to the area.

The end result was the largest earth filled dam in the world at the time. The building material used, was the rock and earth piles created by the gold dredging which lined the riverbanks for miles. The material was transported by a special railroad constructed for that purpose. The end result was a 770 ft. high dam, (the tallest in the United States) creating a 690 ft. deep lake with 167 miles of shoreline, with an incredible recreational area for anyone who owned a boat or had friends that did.

A Double Minded Man

I was the third child of four children. I had one brother, six years older than I, whom I idolized as well as two sisters. One sister was two years older and one, two years younger.

My father was an unskilled worker with an eighth grade education, who along with my mother, was raised in the Ozark Mountains of northern Arkansas. They eloped and came to California in search of an opportunity during World War II. My father was rejected from military service due to a heart defect. He found work in the ammunition factories near San Francisco.

After the war they moved to Butte County to work in the rice processing plants of western Butte County and my father eventually landed a job as a janitor, cleaning classrooms at Oroville high school in the evenings.

Mom raised the children. We didn't see much of dad during the week because he worked 3 P.M. to 11 P.M. Dad made sure we had chores to do after school and on Saturday. We always went to church Sunday morning and evening.

I guess we were poor, but it didn't matter most of the time. Dad was a wheeler dealer. He was always buying and selling something for a profit after he had my brother and I repair or re-

The Early Years

model it. Dad taught all the kids how to hunt and fish. We never went without food and our freezer was always full.

During the summers, my mother took us to the orchards, where we picked prunes, peaches, olives, tomatoes, apricots, almonds and walnuts with the migrant farm workers to supplement our family income and buy new school clothes and supplies. We were always encouraged to eat all the fruit and nuts we could when we were working.

Sometimes my dad would take my brother and I to the old gold fields and we would collect a pickup load of discarded scrap iron and take it to a salvage yard where we might get five dollars.

Even though I grew up within a 5 mile radius of Oroville, we lived in a different house every year. This was because my dad would find a bargain priced home that needed renovating and we would move in and provide the free labor to remodel it. Every member of the family was required to paint, landscape, roof or do whatever was needed until it was finished. Dad's home-improvement projects usually took about one year. Then the house was sold for a profit and we moved to another project and repeated the process.

As a result, I became very handy and learned the value of hard work at an early age. If something was broke, we fixed it. I don't ever remember a repair man being called to our house for anything. We were taught to be self sufficient.

Although I was very social at school, I didn't participate in extracurricular activities or team sports. This was not because I didn't want to or was not athletic, but because I always had after school jobs. In my family, if you wanted anything beyond the basic necessities, you had to pay for them yourself. Thus, I always had part-time jobs after school.

Since I couldn't commit to team sports, my athletic endeavors were limited to track and field and boxing. These events required only my efforts and I didn't have to rely on anyone else and no-one else had to rely on me. I was naturally fast and won most of my fist fights so these two activities didn't require any special effort on my part. Because of my upbringing, I knew how to work with my hands, so my favorite subjects in school were auto shop, wood shop, metal shop, welding and girls.

Growing up during the era of hot rods and

muscle cars (after I could legally drive) I managed to have some of the coolest cars in the high school parking lot.

A lot of moving violation tickets were also accumulated and my driver's license was suspended for a period of time. By the time I graduated from high school I had bought, fixed up and sold a dozen cars.

People often ask how I ended up in law-enforcement. Well, it wasn't a desire of mine. In fact all of my law-enforcement encounters had not left a positive impression on my life.

After high school, my smart classmates went to places like Cal Berkeley, Stanford, and UC Davis. Even though I always maintained a B average in school, I had no scholarship and my family had no funds to provide a college education for me or my siblings.

My older brother joined the Navy. My older sister dropped out of school at age 16 and got married. After the three of us were gone my parents sent my youngest sister to college, where she met and married her soul mate.

After high school graduation, my father told me I was a "grown-up" and if I wanted to contin-

A Double Minded Man

ue living at home I needed to pay rent. Not wanting to do that, I found and purchased my first home, an 8' x 33' trailer, which I parked next to my white Corvette and thought I would become a swinging free love bachelor.

The Early Years

A Double Minded Man

-3-

JOB CHANGE

It seemed only right that I should go to the local junior college and continue my education. After all, isn't that what we are all programmed to do by the government system? Go to school, get a good education, get a good job and work till you die.

I've since come to believe after acquiring two college degrees and attending law school, that the A students teach B students, who are employed by C students.

I also believe that our public school system and colleges are simply businesses. They exist to provide jobs and benefits for the faculty and staff and after you graduate and stop paying tuition, they have no interest in you or your success.

A Double Minded Man

Junior-college felt like a continuation of high school to me. I signed up for an electrical engineering program as a major, only because the college counselor said I had to have a declared major. It was the only thing I could think of at the time as I remembered my brother taking a few electrical engineering classes before he joined the Navy. I didn't even know what an electrical engineer was or did.

In addition to attending junior college, I supported myself by working at night at a full-service gas station, pumping gas and doing light mechanical repair 30 to 40 hours per week.

The gas station just happened to be next to the California State Police substation. During shift change, all the officers pulled their cruisers into my station for fuel and service. Since I wasn't a fan of the police, I soon figured that whenever I needed gas for my personal car, I would just add one dollar on to each officers' gas bill. After all, they didn't pay any attention and just paid with a California State credit card. I carefully kept track of the additional charges and at the end of my shift, I simply pulled my Corvette up to the pump and filled my tank with the high-octane gasoline that the police paid for. It was my way of payback and it worked pretty well for about a year.

Job Change

Over time, I became pretty well acquainted with a young patrolman by the name of Hal Yowell. Hal was a cool guy in his mid 20s. He often shared with me interesting stories about his work or things that happened during his shift of duty. He even took me and my girlfriend at the time, Mic (who later became my forever wife), skiing on Lake Oroville with his young family.

One evening, as I was getting ready to close the station, Hal pulled in to gas up his police cruiser. After making small talk, he asked if I ever considered going into law enforcement.

"No way, I said."

"Well I think it would be a good profession for a guy like you," replied Hal.

"I haven't got a very good history with the police," I responded.

"Well I see from your police record you like to drive fast and you could do that legally in a police car," said Hal.

"No thanks. Besides, I'm going to be an engineer."

Hal didn't know three weeks prior to that I had really been struggling with my engineering classes. A high school friend, who was in a pre-law program at the same junior college, told me that in his program, all they did was read court cases and sit around and talk about them.

A Double Minded Man

I quickly decided that was the kind of college curriculum for me, so at the end of the quarter, I switched my educational major to pre-law.

Hal continued, "Well Glenn, I think you should consider law-enforcement as a possible profession. You're in good physical condition. You're smart. You like fast cars. You won't get rich, but you can make a good living and earn enough money to pay for your own gas for your car."

I couldn't believe what I was hearing. At first I pretended I didn't know what he was talking about but it was no use. I was busted.

Hal went on to say, "You think you are pretty smart. I've been on to you for a long time, so here's the deal: you can go to jail or next week, you can go to Sacramento, submit an application and take the entrance aptitude exam for the California State Police." He then handed me an application form.

The following week found me sitting in a state building in Sacramento with about 25 other applicants taking a two hour exam, which I passed with a score of 93.

Two weeks after that, I was taking a medical

Job Change

exam and a physical agility test.

Three weeks later at the age of 21 and three days into marriage to my wife Mic, I reported to a 10 week training academy in West Sacramento to become a member of the California State Police.

Hal Yowell and I remained close friends until his death from cancer at the age of 37.

A Double Minded Man

-4-

STATE POLICE

I remember my first day in a patrol car by myself. It was an old Plymouth Satellite. I tested the radio, the lights and siren. I was hoping for a Code 3 opportunity; a chance to travel in an emergency situation: lights flashing, siren blaring, perhaps a high speed pursuit. After all, what good is all that Law Enforcement training if you don't get to use it? But my shift turned out to be boring and uneventful. Mostly assisting motorists with vehicle problems.

However, as darkness began to fall, I received a radio call of a man down near the I-5 and W. Capital Rd. in Sacramento. I imagined it was a murder victim, a hit and run, or a crime scene. As I responded to the call, I rolled up to the site, sure enough, there was a male "victim" lying on the highway easement in the dry grass. Apparently reported by an anonymous traveler.

My mind was racing. I was cautious as I approached the "lifeless" body, a male. He appeared to be homeless and dirty, in his 40's with a backpack lying nearby. I was careful not to disturb a "crime scene." There was no visible blood and he definitely looked dead.

I radioed in the situation to the dispatcher, the shift Sergeant came on the radio stating he would respond.

I began to set out a few road flares to block off the 3rd lane of traffic and protect the scene. Sergeant Dunn was a statistic: divorced, ex-wife and kids somewhere, 30 pounds overweight and out of shape. His uniform shirt buttons strained to contain his stomach. Too many donuts and coffee, too much time sitting in a police car.

After I explained the situation to Sergeant Dunn, I asked if I should take pictures and call an ambulance. Sergeant Dunn was silent and slowly walked around the "obviously dead victim."

Finally he asked if I checked his vitals. I explained that I had poked him with my flash light and there had been no response. Sergeant Dunn

State Police

then kneeled down over the body, looking it up and down. He then stood up and looked around the area slowly. He walked a few feet away and picked up a liter bottle of Gallo wine that still contained a small amount of liquid and glanced back at me and said nothing.

Sergeant Dunn then walked slowly back to the "victim" and quickly gave him two swift kicks in the ass and yelled, "Get up asshole." I was horrified. Suddenly the "lifeless" body on the ground gasped, moaned and sat up.

I wished I could say I had witnessed a miracle, a healing, a man brought back from the dead, but no—I simply saw a drunk, homeless man awakened from his stupor.

Sergeant Dunn walked up to me and slowly shook his head. I was speechless and humiliated. As the Sergeant slowly walked back to his patrol car he barked, "Fill out an incident report, clean up these flares and meet me at the Denny's in 30 minutes." "Yes Sir", I said. I felt like Barney Fife from the Andy Griffith TV Show.

Sergeant Dunn became very influential to me during the 5 years I spent under his command. Obviously, my first lesson was things are not always what they seem. I learned street smarts and that rules and policy from manuals don't always work in real life situations. He was extremely protective of the officers he supervised. Even though he was gruff and tough, he never criticized officers in front of others.

Sergeant Dunn encouraged me to finish college and attend law school and even join the Secret Service. He always said "You don't want to end up like me, do you?"

I regret that I lost contact with him after the Secret Service began to move me around. Sergeant Dunn was my first real mentor.

State Police

A Double Minded Man

MY FAMILY

The first time I saw her, I was enchanted. She pulled into the full service Chevron station (yes, the same one next to the State Police Substation) and asked for two dollars worth of gas. As I washed her windshield, I couldn't help noticing how beautiful she was. Long dark hair, busty, with great legs. I had never seen her before and in a small town like Oroville, she would be hard to miss.

As she handed me her two dollars, I smiled at her. She smiled back, said, "Thank you," and quickly drove away. I asked several people about her, but nobody seemed to know who she was.

Two nights later, she was back in my station, driving the same blue Mercury and asked for two dollars worth of gas. I spent an extra amount of time cleaning her windshield so I could discreetly look her over good. She seemed indifferent to my attention to her. I was captivated and determined to make her acquaintance, but she handed me two dollars and sped away.

The following Saturday, Oroville was having its annual Feather Fiesta Day Parade. I had nothing better to do, so I stood on a downtown curb with a friend and watched the high school bands, horses, and makeshift floats roll by.

Lo and behold, there she was! The girl from the gas station. She had been taken captive by the local Rotary Club and was being held in a make shift jail on the back of a flatbed truck. It was a fund raiser, where people were grabbed and put in "jail" until someone posted their bail. I had $20, that I intended to party with over the weekend. But this was my chance.

Running after the truck, I waved my $20 bill in the air. The Rotary truck finally came to a halt. One of their members gladly accepted my $20 donation and released the two dollar beauty from custody.

Her name was Mickie, but she went by Mic. She told me she was 18, but I later found out she was only 17. Mic was attending beauty college.

My Family

She had graduated early from the same high school I attended, but I had never seen her.

She came from a family of unskilled construction laborers, who had moved from Alaska to work on the Oroville Dam project. Shortly after arriving in Oroville, her mother and stepfather divorced.

One evening, her mother, a party girl, was enjoying herself in a local bar while Mic and her brothers were left at home alone (this was a regular occurrence). A fight broke out inside the bar between two local men. One of the men went outside to his car and retrieved a shotgun to improve his odds. The end result was, Mic's mother, a bystander, received a face full of buckshot and was left totally blind at the age of 28. Mic was 10 years old at the time, but found herself not only caring for her mother, but also raising her three younger brothers. They survived on welfare benefits.

As a result, Mic was deprived of a childhood and had no time for socializing, dating or school activities. She went to school, work, cooked, cleaned and became a nurse and caretaker of her mother and brothers. That's why none of my associates knew the identity of this, 5'7" shapely, dark-haired beauty. She obtained a special drivers license at age 14 and graduated high school at 16.

A year later we were married in a local outdoor park. Mic made her own dress and we paid for everything. We took a short two day trip (which we called a honeymoon) along the coast of Northern California. Three days after the wedding, we towed our 33 foot trailer to a trailer park in West Sacramento, where I began my State Police career. We were poor, but we were in love and determined to make it.

Five years later, we had a daughter Tessa, who I have always referred to as my Star. I wanted to name her Star, but was overruled. She is a total sanguine, who lights up every room she enters. Her main goal in life is to have fun. Everyone loves Tessa.

Three years later, we had a son named Dustin, who I wanted to call Cord, but again, I was overruled. Dustin was a very active and athletic child, but has a very short attention span. Today he would be diagnosed with A.D.D.

Dustin, like Tessa, is also very outgoing and independent. He can't stand the environment of corporate America or the world of desks and cubicles. Therefore, he has always worked in sales.

My Family

He is independent and wants to get paid based on his own performance, not what someone else thinks he is worth.

Both Tessa and Dustin are adults now, married to wonderful spouses with children of their own. People who know them are fortunate to have them as their friends. I am so proud of them both.

Of course, I am full of remorse and regret not being there for them, being a better father to them and missing so much of their childhood.

The Secret Service is not conducive to family life. Very few agents, who come in married, leave married. The long separation, the travel, the temptations and opportunities take their toll. Infidelity is a common practice, especially when traveling abroad.

Mic always made it very clear that anything I needed was available at home. Plus, I'm sure she had plenty of opportunities and temptations herself. We had also made the promise, we would never, ever, vocalize the "D" word (divorce). No matter how rough things were, we committed to work it out. Anybody can quit on their marriage. It takes commitment to make it work.

Mic's childhood was terrible. Her mother, even though blind, married five different men, most of who were drunks and abusive. Many atrocities occurred in her home. Mic does not know who her real father is and to this day rarely speaks of her childhood and chooses to repress those experiences and keep looking forward. After all these years, I'm still married to that gorgeous brunette Mic and still madly in love with her.

Every day I tell her "I'm a lucky guy." She says "yes you are." Once in a while, she even tells me "she's a lucky girl."

My Family

A Double Minded Man

-6-

BASICS

Even though I was raised in a small town in Northern California, using and respecting firearms had been a part of my upbringing. Our household contained an assortment of handguns as well as shotguns and rifles for hunting. However, if we weren't going to eat a living creature, we didn't kill it. That was the rule. That rule did not apply however, to stray dogs or neighbor's cats that threatened our household pets.

I was not naïve when I joined the US Secret Service. I had worked for the California Department of Justice while completing college and had been a California State Police Officer for five years.

Isn't it amazing how we make decisions that affect our lives and those around us without any real thought or study about the lifelong consequences?

In the case of the USSS, I had never considered what the special agent position offered, what it entailed, or what it could lead to in my life. At that time, I had a mortgage, wife, daughter, and dog and was attending law school in my off time from the State Police. One day my sergeant, for whom I had great respect called me aside after a shift briefing. Sergeant Dunn had been a police officer for 29 years and was going to retire in seven months. I had earned his respect by simply doing my job effectively and correctly; nothing more. Sergeant Dunn knew I had higher aspirations and asked me if I wanted to end up like him? What could I say? So I remained silent. He told me his neighbor was a high level supervisor in the Secret Service and he could arrange for me to have an interview.

I had very little knowledge as to the complete job description of a Secret Service Agent, but I thought this might be an interesting possibility.

The next week, after completing a graveyard shift with the State Police, I found myself wearing an ill fitting suit purchased from JCPenney and sitting in front of a stern, no-nonsense Secret Service Agent, whose desk name tag said George McCarthy ASAIC (Assistant Special Agent In-

Basics

Charge). He asked me a series of question about my family, education, work experience, drug use and personal beliefs.

He then told me to come back to his office in two days at 8 a.m. to take a general aptitude test.

I arrived exhausted. Having a crying daughter with an ear infection in the room adjacent to where you are trying to sleep in the daytime does not work. I had also just completed a graveyard work shift involving a high-speed chase, which had ended in a terrible car crash in which two people were critically injured. Because of all the paperwork I had to complete concerning the crash, I was frazzled and stressed, arriving 30 minutes late for the test. McCarthy did not seem pleased that I was late, but seemed OK with my reason.

He then ushered me into an adjoining conference room. He gave me two sharp #2 pencils, placed a 30 page paper booklet in front of me, a multiple choice answers sheet and told me to get started. Expecting a room full of other applicants to be tested, imagine my surprise when I realized I was being given a private written exam.

I was wiped out. The exam took me almost 3 hours to complete. I barely passed and I could tell McCarthy was not impressed. Afterwards they scheduled me to come back for a panel interview.

I had been through this before with the State Police and a couple other police departments for which I had applied. This interview occurred in the same conference room as before and consisted of myself seated across the table from four experienced S.S. Agents. I spent the next 45 minutes responding to their questions about everything from my sex life to every dishonest thing I had ever done or thought about doing that I could remember. In addition, the panel would introduce hypothetical events and situations to me and question my response and why.

Fortunately for me, I had not worked the previous two days and felt rested and ready for this interview. I thought my responses were good and I could tell from their expressions that they did also.

Next I was scheduled for a psychological examination and a polygraph test. The psychological examination consisted of me making an appointment the next week at a medical clinic where I had to fill out a bunch of forms about my medical history. I then was interviewed by a hippie looking guy wearing a white medical

Basics

smock that smelled like tobacco and claimed to be a psychiatrist. He wanted to know how I felt about my father, mother, siblings, coworkers, former teachers, prejudices and people in general. He also gave me a series of spoken words and wanted me to verbally respond with the first word that came to mind. Such as "sky = blue, black = white." I was also shown a series of ink blots and asked what I saw.

I never got to see the results or know what his evaluation said, but I guess I passed, because I was soon scheduled for my polygraph examination, which occurred in the Secret Service conference room again.

I had never taken a polygraph test and was quite nervous about it. After being introduced to the man administering the exam and an agent I knew from the panel interview, I was seated in a hard wooden chair with no padding. Sensors were attached to my index fingers and a monitor was strapped around my chest. Also, a sensor was taped to my forehead. I was told to stare straight ahead and focus at the blank wall. I could feel sweat breaking out on my forehead. I took a few deep breaths and tried to relax.

I was then asked four or five innocuous questions such as: Is your name John Smith? Were you born in California? Are you 26 years old? I was told these questions are to test the equipment. I could hear the needles scratching the paper in response to my answers. Next were the real questions. Questions like: Have you ever been a member of an anti-American group? Have you ever participated in a protest? Have you ever used an illegal drug? Have you ever had sexual relationships with another male? Etc. Etc.

Even though I was truthful in my responses and knew I gave the correct answer, every time I heard the needles scratching the paper on the polygraph machine I was unnerved.

Next came months and months of waiting and silence. The agency conducted background checks and interviewed current and past neighbors, coworkers, classmates and former teachers and family members. Agents even came to the house on two occasions and interviewed my wife.

Eventually I was sent to a medical doctor and given a complete physical examination. After another month of nothing, I received a call from ASAIC McCarthy scheduling an appointment to come to my house and meet with my wife and me.

Basics

McCarthy was there to offer me a position as a special agent with the U.S. Secret Service. The agent position was in San Francisco. I was told it would be the only offer I would ever receive and had 48 hours to decide. The starting salary was about $5000 less than I was earning annually as a California State Police Officer. If I wanted the job, I would have 60 days to report to San Francisco.

Even though my original plan had been to complete law school, take the bar exam, and go to work for the district attorney's office. Mic and I decided this might be an interesting diversion for a couple of years and would look good on a future resume.

Little did I know about what lay ahead and what was in store for me.

A Double Minded Man

-7-

TRAINING

FLETC, the Federal Law Enforcement Training Center, in Glynco, Georgia, is the basic federal law enforcement training facility that is attended by most federal law officers, and provides both classroom education and field exercises. Our class consisted of Secret Service, US Deputy Marshals, Customs Agents, IRS, and some Border Patrol. Secret Service Agents had their own dormitory building, exclusive of everyone else. There was no Homeland Security at that time. The FBI trained their own people in Quantico, Virginia.

Everyone wore the same dark blue pants and light blue shirt. We looked like mechanics or gas station attendants. The same academic and physical requirements were placed on everyone. FLETC wasn't really a challenge for me compared to the California State Police Academy.

    Glynco, Georgia is a small town. The Federal Law Enforcement Training Center is situated on what had formerly been an Army installation. The area is flat and wooded, covered with pine trees and dotted with numerous small lakes. I was always on the lookout for snakes and alligators, but I never saw either around the training facility. The main opportunities for employment in Glynco were provided by the numerous paper mills surrounding the area. The sour smell coming from wood pulp processing at the paper mills was repulsive and constant. We were not allowed family visits the entire 10 weeks of the basic training academy. As you would expect, a few agents, feeling lonely, bored, and working hard, developed romantic sexual relationships with others attending the academy. I tried to control my own urges with running and exercise. I missed my beautiful wife.

    Monday through Friday, our days began at 6 a.m. with roll call, then marching military style, followed by breakfast, which was also served military style. Breakfast was the same food every day; scrambled eggs, oatmeal, potatoes, sausage or bacon, pancakes, toast, dry cereal, milk coffee or orange juice. We could eat whatever we wanted. Breakfast was followed by class-

Training

room instruction on everything from search and seizure rules, constitutional law, habeas corpus, arrest procedure and first aid.

Lunches were cold cut sandwiches, iceberg lettuce salad, or burgers. My favorite thing about lunch was the freezer full of various ice cream bars.

Afternoons usually consisted of physical fitness training, firearms training, self defense, and practical arrest or search and seizure warrant exercises. Some of these were quite physical and injuries happened frequently. If agents were injured badly, they were sent back to their home office until they recovered. They were then free to return to FLETC, but had to start over with the next training class.

I determined that I was not going to get sick or injured.

After satisfactorily completing basic training we were each sent back to our home agencies. For some of the graduates, their training was complete. But Secret Service agents were now assigned to a senior agent mentor for six months at their field office.

Following that, agents would be sent to Washington, D.C. for 12 weeks of specialized Secret Service training at D.C. headquarters and Beltsville, Maryland. Each agent was allowed $50 a day living expenses. With that money we were expected to acquire some form of lodging, pay for all of our food and essentials for the next 12 weeks. Although impractical, our family could stay with us.

The only requirement was that we show up every morning where assigned, either the D.C. headquarters training facility or Beltsville, Maryland at the designated time, generally 7 a.m. Dress code was business casual of your choice. No jeans or T-shirts.

We were taught specialized hand to hand combat, first aid and CPR, how to safely use, maintain, and handle a variety of firearms including handguns, shotguns, rifles and automatic weapons.

We studied how genuine currency and coins are manufactured from the raw material to the finished product. We became experts in distinguishing genuine American money from counterfeit. Learned about handwriting, forgery, and questioned document. We learned how to pick locks and how to survive without food or water supplies. We also studied every successful and

Training

unsuccessful presidential assassination attempt in recent history and dissected every aspect of what went wrong and what could have been done better.

In protection training, we trained in every possible position and formation with a protectee; walking, running, parades, motorcades, rope lines, and crowd control. We were placed in every kind of situation to see how we would respond. Each live, expertly simulated exercise was filmed and later evaluated with instructors.

We were attacked by lone gunmen, multiple attackers and assassins. We were attacked by vehicles, and coped with live explosions. We were trained on how to handle a 12,000 pound armor plated limousine in a crisis situation. The training was intense and covered every possible scenario and made as realistic as possible using Hollywood type sets, props and even a real airplane.

In time our responses in these situations became instinctive and automatic. We acted or reacted without thinking. In a real life situation, you don't have time to figure out a response. It has to be instantaneous and correct. The wrong response will get you a congressional inquiry and a life of regret.

It was a proud day when we graduated, were issued our commission book, badge, and were sworn in. We were also issued our personal firearm, handcuffs, and custom-fitted, bulletproof vest. They even gave us a briefcase and sunglasses.

I felt invincible and as though I was ready to take on the villains of the world.

I was a Secret Service Agent.

Training

A Double Minded Man

-§-

THE PADDED ROOM

I had heard about the infamous Padded Room from other agents in my office. No one would ever elaborate about what took place there. They would simply say something along the lines of, "wait 'til you get to the Padded Room." One day during a physical training exercise we were brought into an open area with mats on the floor.

Our training instructor put us through a series of basic calisthenics and stretching maneuvers for about 15 minutes. Then, one by one, people were called to another room - The Padded Room.

I never saw the people who went in there come back out. Everything was very quiet as we waited.

Now it was my turn to go through the door.

A Double Minded Man

The room was about 20' x 20'. It had padding on the floor and on all of the walls. It had a strong, dank locker room smell. My heart was pounding and I could feel myself starting to sweat. A single instructor waited inside wearing military style lace-up boots, loose fitting black nylon pants and a tight black shirt with the word "Instructor" in gold lettering across the chest. He was lean and muscular and his head was shaved. He definitely had that no-nonsense don't-mess with-me look.

He asked if I had ever been in a fistfight. I answered truthfully that I had been in a few fights in my day.

"Great," he said, "we're going to spar a couple of rounds just to make sure you know how to handle yourself."

I was relieved. I had been a California State Police Officer for five years prior to this, and had boxed Golden Gloves for a number of years in high school and junior college. I knew how to handle myself in a boxing ring. In fact, I might open up a can of whoop-ass on this guy if he started to play rough. This was going to be no big deal.

We put on protective headgear and "boxing gloves," which were no more than snow mittens.

The Padded Room

They definitely did not fit the description of boxing gloves. I wondered what kind of boxing we'd be doing. We began to dance around the room and throw a few punches at each other. Certainly nothing serious and no hard blows were landed.

After two or three minutes of this, the instructor said, "We're gonna notch it up now. No kicking. No hitting below the belt. No punching in the face."

The words "I understand" barely made it out of my mouth when a bolt of lightning hit me and I hit the floor, disbelief and confusion flooding my brain. I'd been dealt a violent kick to the groin. A wave of nausea overwhelmed me. He instantly grabbed me by the hair and punched me again and again in the face. Blood poured from my nose and mouth and flew everywhere with each punch.

He stood up and yelled "Get up!" I tried to push myself up, but he kicked me in the ribs with his heavy boot and screamed obscenities at me, "Get up you fucking pussy." I could not breathe. I was close to passing out. The blows to my face and body did not stop, and I began to think that he meant to kill me. Next he was bellowing profanities about my wife and mother, kicking me, punching me, and screaming at me to get up.

Then I saw red. Before his next kick I swung around and caught that bastard's boot in my hands and violently twisted it, knocking him off his feet. Instantly I was on top of him, beating his face in with both fists, giving him everything I had.

The side door of the room instantly banged open and two guys rushed in yelling for me to stop. One of them tackled me, bellowing, "Stop, you passed!" With rage and pain and blood blinding me, I shouted "Passed? What are you talking about?"

As he let me go and got up, he said "Calm down buddy, it was an exercise. We needed to see what you'd do, how you'd react in a life or death situation." I let out a laugh that was part disbelief and part fury. The other one tossed me a damp towel and chimed in, "And see if you'd get back up after you got knocked down."
"Yeah?" I panted, wiping my bleeding face with shaky hands, "What happens if they don't get up? Do you shoot them?" "Nah, they're done. They go home," he replied.

I've often wondered if the Training Division still puts trainees through that exercise. I hope they do, but I imagine the bleeding hearts probably discontinued it long ago.

The Padded Room

I have reflected on that life lesson and asked myself: if I am hurt, in pain, bleeding, or shot or stabbed would I just lie there if my partner were dying? If the President was being killed, when all hell is breaking loose--what are you going to do when life knocks you down? Lie there or get back up and fight?

I think it was Sylvester Stallone in a "Rocky" movie that said, "It's not how hard you can hit that matters, but how hard you can get hit and get back up that counts."

A Double Minded Man

-9-

RUBEN

Sometimes the training sessions were more dangerous and detrimental than real life experiences.

Ruben Gomez was one of my best friends. He and I were hired on the same day. He was from the Miami field office and had been my roommate during basic training in Georgia. We both had come from similar low income, but good families. His parents had fled Cuba when Fidel Castro became its dictator.

We both loved muscle cars and had beautiful wives that we loved. We became good friends in Georgia and spent most of our off time studying and checking out the local sites together.

During one of our training sessions at the Secret Service academy in Beltsville, Maryland, an accident occurred which would forever change Ruben's destiny.

During motorcade movements at slow speed, the agent runs alongside the armored limousine occupied by the President. Four agents position themselves on the corners of the limousine. There are also running boards that extend beyond the sides of the vehicle. As the motorcade picks up speed, the agent jumps onto the running boards. As with most things, it is a lot harder than it sounds to jump on and off of a moving vehicle without tripping or falling. There is a proper technique and it requires a lot of practice with an actual armored limousine. With all the armor plating and bulletproof glass, these vehicles weigh 12,000 to 15,000 pounds.

You do not want to get run over by one of these cars. Agents must maintain a safe distance from the vehicle by keeping their extended arm and hand touching the corner of the vehicle at all times, running or walking.

While conducting one of these training exercises, we were experiencing light rain fall. As the limousine was slowing to about 5 mph, Ruben and I were positioned on the passenger side running boards. The shift leader gave the command to hit the ground. As Ruben jumped forward and out to take his position on the right, front fender. His right foot slipped on the wet pavement and the running board struck his left leg knocking him to the ground.

The back wheel of the heavy vehicle then ran over his left foot and ankle. I still remember the sound of his ankle bones crushing under the heavyweight of the armored limousine.

Ruben had to leave the Secret Service before he actually got started. He ended up having his entire ankle fused into one immovable piece.

He eventually joined his father in his cable television business and became a very successful businessman.

Ruben and I still talk a couple times a year and send each other Christmas cards.

A Double Minded Man

-10-

BORIS

Every organization has its unique characters - people who stand out, people who are even legendary. The San Francisco Field office had several.

Being a newly hired rookie after 12 weeks of basic Federal law enforcement training at Glynco, Georgia, I was assigned to a senior agent for on the job training for six months. I was assigned to Boris Ebert. Boris was a legend. Most agents were intimidated by him. He had played professional football for the New England Patriots as a defensive linebacker. Boris was huge in many ways, 6'4" and close to 300 pounds. He had a deep voice with a New England accent. Boris hated everybody equally. Everything that came out of his mouth was politically incorrect. Boris referred to everybody in ethnic terms. "That

A Double Minded Man

Nigger, that Jew, that Gook, that Greaser." You get the idea.

Boris was also fearless. He gained his legendary status when he worked in the New York field office. Rumor has it that he was working undercover in an organized crime sting operation that went bad. When the deal went bad, Boris was unarmed. The bad guys weren't. They were next to a swimming pool. Boris tackled them football style, taking two of them into the swimming pool where he broke their necks and drowned them. When backup finally arrived, a third accomplice was found dead with the handle of a pool cleaning brush jammed through his chest. The whole incident was hushed up and did not get into the media's hands.

Boris was given the moniker of "Pool Man" and transferred to San Francisco, which he affectionately referred to as "Fag City." No one called Boris "Pool Man" to his face.

Much to Boris' displeasure, he was ordered to be my coach and trainer for the next six months. Boris wasn't happy. He liked to do his own thing and didn't give a damn about policy or proper procedure. He got results his way and it usually wasn't neat and tidy. Normally an agent's career track consists of 3 to 5 years in a criminal field

Boris

office, followed by a 3 to 5 year assignment in Washington, D.C. protecting the President or Vice President, then back to a field office. Boris had been on the job 11 years with no permanent protective assignment. I guess the powers that be felt it was better for everyone to keep Boris in the field. That suited him fine as he often referred to the agents assigned to protective details as "pretty boys in suits."

When I was first brought into Boris' office and introduced as his trainee, he stood up and said, "Like hell. I ain't training this little faggot," and walked out of his office to the SAIC's office. As I sat in his office alone, I observed his walls had semi nude pictures of female models holding guns in seductive poses, and a banner that said "San Francisco is a sucking hole of despair." You could see that New York had been crossed out and replaced with San Francisco.

Five minutes later, Boris stormed back into his office, slammed the door shut and stood towering over my foot 5 foot 10 inch frame scowling at me.

"Let's get a few things straight," he roared. I'm not happy about this. I don't like you and I'm not your friend. Do what I say and stay out of my way. You better not fuck up. Is that clear?"

A Double Minded Man

I thought I was standing in front of a Marine drill sergeant. "Yes sir," I said.

"Get out of my office."

And that's how my partnership with Boris Ebert began.

Boris was a "the end justifies the means" kind of guy. The first time he invited me to ride along with him it was to interview a victim/witness in the East Bay city of Oakland California. On the drive over from San Francisco across the Oakland Bay Bridge, he said, "Forget all that crap you learned at FLETC (Federal Law Enforcement Training Center). The real world doesn't follow policy or rules of engagement. Those might apply to some pencil neck faggot who sits behind a desk and pushes paper all day, but those guys wouldn't survive a week on the streets."

As we parked on the street in front of a three-story brick government project building, I could see this was no place for a blond haired blue-eyed white boy. The building was dilapidated. Trash was everywhere. Graffiti covered the walls and several black males stared at us with disdain and hatred. As we walked past two men at the doorway, one of them muttered, "honky pigs." I was glad to be with Boris.

Boris

The inside of the building was dark, with the exception of a flickering light bulb dangling from a bare wire in the staircase. The smell was putrid, like something was dead. We slowly climbed the filthy trash strewn stairs. The stench got worse. As we approached the second floor landing and looked down the hallway, 20 feet from where we stood, we saw what appeared to be a teenage male sitting motionless on the floor with his back to the wall. It soon became obvious where the terrible odor was coming from. The bloated male had a bullet hole in his forehead. Dried blood held him in position

I had never seen a dead body outside of a funeral home. Not only was the site horrifying, but the smell was gut-wrenching. I covered my face with the sleeve of my jacket and fought the urge to vomit.

"What shall we do," I ask. Boris cautiously looked up and down the hall then said, "Let's go! We aren't here for this."

I thought he meant let's get out of here. Instead, we proceeded up the stairs to the third-floor. Boris knocked on door 3C and stood to the side. After Boris banged on the door two or three more times, an elderly female voice inside asked, "Who's there?" After waiting for her to unlock four deadbolts, we were admitted.

Mrs. Davis was a widow. A dark skinned black woman in her mid-70s. She lived alone with her golden colored cat. Her late husband had been dead almost five years; however, the social security office had not been notified and had continued to send out his monthly payment checks, which were subsequently forged and cashed.

These kinds of low level cases are what rookie S.S. Agents are assigned to investigate. They are rarely prosecuted, because the US attorney's office has bigger things to deal with. However, these cases give needed street investigative experience and take agents into places and situations that force them to live or die. Boris was giving me some basic training. I was there to watch and learn.

As Boris sat at the dirty kitchen table interviewing the woman, she calmly sat across from him and proceeded to straighten her frizzy hair with a hot metal rod that she heated on an open gas flame on her stove. The stench of the singed hair was horrible. However, after what I had experienced on the second floor, this was nothing.

As I looked around, I was glad to be standing. Cat hair and fur balls were everywhere. Soon the cat began to rub against my leg. I gently pushed it aside, so it decided to try Boris' legs under the table. I watched with amusement as Boris attempted to kick the persistent cat aside. Finally Boris slowly reached under the table with his right hand and grabbed the cat by the neck. As Boris continued to question the lady, I heard faint crunching sounds and Boris dropped the cats limp body to the floor and continued the questioning without interruption.

After taking handwriting samples from Mrs. Davis it was obvious she had forged and cashed the checks and although admitting she had done so, did not feel she had done anything wrong. As we were descending the stairs, I wanted to ask Boris about the cat. However, when we reached the ground floor landing we were met by three black males. One was holding an aluminum baseball bat. It was obvious this was not a welcoming committee and was not going to end well. My heart was pounding.

"What can I do for you boys?" Boris calmly said.
"You did not pay rent to use my building," the man holding the bat replied.
"I'm sorry," said Boris and instantly slammed his right knuckles into the man's throat crushing

his windpipe. He dropped the baseball bat with a loud clanking noise and crumpled to the floor gasping for air.

Boris then turned his attention to the other two men who were out of arms reach. They turned and ran. Boris then stepped over the man on the ground and said, "Let's get out of this shithole."

I never asked Boris about the cat. I decided right then, Boris was now my new best friend.

I learned a lot from Boris. Always strike first. Don't wait to get hit and then act. It's too late then. Never fight fair. The goal is to stay alive. Take your opponent out as quickly as possible or slow them down enough so you can run away. Never hit anybody with a clenched fist. It will just bust up your hand.

It wasn't usually pretty but Boris got the job done and had the respect of every field agent who knew him.

The SAIC in the San Francisco office personally read every rookie agent's activity and investigative reports. At first every report submitted, no matter how accurate or thoroughly it had been prepared, would come back with a large three inch red ink stamp which read, "BULLSHIT".

Boris

Below that would be the handwritten word "redo." After a few times painstakingly rewriting the entire report that was already accurate, I finally realized that this was simply a powerplay on his part.

Boris finally told me to simply resubmit the same report with a new cover page to replace the "BULLSHIT" stamp and it would be accepted. This scenario was obviously the boss' way of letting you know who was in charge the first year on the job.

A Double Minded Man

-11-

THE DOBERMAN

It was a big day. A whole year had passed since I had been hired as a Secret Service Agent. No longer a Rookie (actually the last guy hired is always called a rookie until someone is hired after them). I was on my own. No training agent. No longer on probation. Fully trained. I had met or exceeded all the standards and requirements placed on me that 1st year on the job and was now ready to enforce all the federal statutes spelled out in Title 18 of the U.S. Criminal Code.

I had a government issued car, gas credit card, briefcase, raid jacket, baseball cap, hand gun, ammo, a booklet of airline tickets for travel, handcuffs, a faux mahogany metal desk with a nameplate…Hell, I even had government issued sunglasses. I also had a stack of unsolved felony cases assigned for me to investigate.

In normal circumstances, S.S. Agents assigned to criminal field offices normally work alone unless backup is needed or it's time to arrest someone.

I was in Richmond, California, a tough, mostly black, oil refinery town in the East Bay a little north of Berkeley. I was following up on a lead - a person of interest in a financial crime case I was investigating. His last known address was in Richmond.

It was about 8 a.m., the area was covered in heavy morning San Francisco Bay area fog. As I drove slowly through the area it was obvious this was a tough neighborhood, which consisted of small, unkept homes with bars on the windows and non-operable vehicles in front yards.

As I parked in front of the house, I observed that a 4 ft. chain link fence surrounded the yard. This house had been converted into a duplex. The yard was covered with dog turds and stunk like urine. As I slowly moved along the sidewalk toward the first unit, I saw it. A large black Doberman was lying on a rug in front of the door. "OH CRAP! Good dog," I whispered as I continued forward. The Doberman seemed unconcerned with me and it didn't move, but I could see its eyes were wide open and staring at me. I sighed with relief when I saw that the number on the door behind the dog was different than what I was looking for. I slowly continued walking toward the back unit, being careful to keep an eye on the Doberman.

As I stood staring at the doorway of the second unit, I realized I would have to open a gate and enter the fence with the Doberman in order to knock on the door. Releasing the latch on the gate, it made a loud metallic sound, which seemed to echo and be amplified in the fog. I quickly looked at the Doberman, but he had no reaction. So I felt he was not a threat.

A window next to the door had a partially opened curtain. I looked in, but it was dark. I could only see the top of a nasty well-worn couch and I thought, "I'm not going to sit on that in my nice dark blue suit," which had been recently purchased off the rack at JCPenney.

I stood to the right of the door and knocked loudly three times. There was nothing. I waited and knocked harder. Still nothing. I was about to reach into my pocket and leave a "call me" card when it happened. Out of the corner of my eye I detected movement.

Silently, flying thru the air like a black panther

was the Doberman. Its mouth was open and its white teeth looked enormous. As I instinctively arched backward the dog struck my shoulder and knocked me off balance and I fell off the porch, landing in the dirt and filth of the yard.

I scrambled to my feet as the dog, now barking and snarling, was regaining its footing for another attack. There was no time to deal with a gate, I leaped over the chain link fence but caught my pant leg tearing a long rip.

I cursed under my breath. I was mortified and furious. Pulling myself together, I looked around to see if anyone had observed this incident. I saw no one, only the Doberman at the fence on its back legs snarling at me. "Go the Hell", I yelled.

To my surprise the dog leaped over the fence and was running straight at me. I pulled my handgun and fired two rounds at the airborne dog from Hell. The dog slammed into me, but at least one of the bullets had landed and the Doberman lay quivering on the ground.

I freaked out, ran to my car and quickly left the area. Trying to think, how am I going to explain this? Should I report this? What repercussion would this create? So much for my first big day off probation!

The Doberman

What does the Secret Service manual say about shooting dogs? Discharging your weapon? Rules of engagement? I was a mental and physical mess. It all happened so fast. What should I do? I needed to think.

Finally I decided to call my old training agent, Boris. He was definitely a "not by the book" guy. As I calmly and with great detail explained the incident to Boris, hoping for wise council, he began to laugh. The more I talked, the louder he laughed! It wasn't funny to me. Finally Boris quit laughing. "What should I do?" I asked. "Your fucked," he said and laughed harder and longer than before. Finally he asked, "Did anybody witness this?" "Not to my knowledge," I answered. Boris then asked, "Did you leave anything behind that could be traced back to you?" "Just blood," I replied.

He pointed out that our government vehicles are registered under fictitious, non-existent corporations. Then after laughing some more, finally said, "If it were me, I would go home, clean up and go back to work and say nothing." Then after more laughter says, "Besides if this story ever got out, you would never live it down. You can do what you want. We never had this conversation." More laughter and then he hung up!

So much for my first day off probation.

I decided to take Boris' advice and hoped for the best. For the next year, every time a supervisor wanted to talk to me, I thought my skeleton was out of the closet. Whenever I saw Boris, he would start laughing.

To this day, whenever I hear the word, Richmond or see a Doberman, my thoughts go back to that incident and sometimes I even laugh.

The Doberman

A Double Minded Man

-12-

SFO FORD

Even though a small percentage of US Secret Service Agents are assigned to protection detail, it is the number one priority of the agency. Everything else is put on hold when protection is needed.

When Gerald Ford was President, he used one of the Harvey Firestone's numerous estates as an escape from Washington, D.C. Even though President Ford was from Grand Rapids, Michigan, his favorite place, which became known as the Western White House, was the Spanish Villa situated on the bluffs of 17-Mile Drive in Carmel, California. I never knew what Ford's ties to Firestone were, but the connection was obviously strong. After Ford left the office of President, he resided in a house next to the Firestone Estate in a private compound on the Thunderbird Golf

A Double Minded Man

Course in Rancho Mirage, an affluent suburb of Palm Springs, California.

Gerald Ford and his family were the first of many presidents I was exposed to. About every three months the San Francisco field office would be notified that President Ford would be visiting his Western White House. That area was under the geographic responsibility of the San Francisco field office. A number of agents would be assigned to assist the Washington, D.C. advance team in making security preparations. I won't go into detail now, but it takes about a week or more to make all the arrangements and coordinate all the logistics anytime the President goes anywhere outside Washington, D.C.

To a limited degree, most field agents didn't mind a break from their investigative casework and there are a lot worse places to spend a few days of your life than "Carmel by the Sea." In fact my wife and I honeymooned there. Ford's activities always included a round of golf at the exclusive Pebble Beach Golf Course.

President Ford had his own set of rules when it came to golf. Since he had been driven everywhere for years in an armored limo, he always insisted on driving his own golf cart. It was his chance to get behind the wheel.

Agents always joked among themselves that President Ford could kick a golf ball 20 yards. If he didn't like where his ball landed, he would simply kick it into a better position. When it comes to golf, I have personally borrowed that golf technique and a few others from President Ford.

The Fords always hosted at least one dinner at the Firestone residence. Guests always included a few local residents including: Dinah Shore, Debbie Reynolds, Tennessee Ernie Ford, Merv Griffin and Clint Eastwood. The agents' personal favorite was obviously Clint Eastwood. Eastwood was in the middle of filming the "Dirty Harry" movie series and was one of the biggest movie stars in the world. He loved the Secret Service and later made several movies portraying a Secret Service Agent. As a result of the "Dirty Harry" movies, Clint Eastwood became a cinematic hero to most people in law enforcement. He often left the dinner parties to visit with the agents.

At the time, Eastwood was in-between wives and would sometimes consume too much alcohol at Ford's dinner parties. At the conclusion, President Ford would walk out to our command post and request an agent to drive Mr. Eastwood home. The senior agents would grumble and swear, because it wasn't in our job description to drive a drunk person home from dinner parties. However, it was a direct request from the President of the United States so what are you going to do?

Being the junior G-man on one occasion, I was given the task. Of course I grumbled and pretended to be unhappy about this. But in reality, I was ecstatic. Can you imagine? Here I am a small town kid, driving Clint Eastwood's bright red Ferrari with Clint Eastwood himself sitting beside me. Not a bad assignment. I had to pinch myself. I've always been a fan of Clint Eastwood on and off the screen.

Needless to say, the job was not always that enjoyable.

SFO Ford

A Double Minded Man

-13-

KENNEDY

In 1979, Senator Ted Kennedy announced he was seeking the Democratic nomination to run against President Jimmy Carter for the 1980 Presidential Election. Also, in 1979, I was transferred from San Francisco to Washington, D.C.

I was already assigned and fulfilling my protection duties in Washington, D.C. However, as a result of the Iranian Embassy crisis; our U.S. Embassy in Tehran had been taken over by Muslim extremists and 60 American citizens were taken captive, tortured, raped and brutalized for 444 straight days. President Carter's response had been to isolate himself at the White House and try to figure out a diplomatic solution. As a result, Secret Service Agents assigned to presidential protection had very little to do since this President did not leave the White House. I, among others was reassigned to some of the candidates seeking the 1980 presidential victory.

I was assigned to Senator Ted Kennedy. Kennedy's reputation was widely known. Although his campaign was disorganized and hurt by lingering questions about Chappaquiddick (where while driving drunk, he put his car into the bay one night and left his female companion there to drown), being a part of his security detail was quite an event.

Because he was a Kennedy and two of his brothers, John and Robert had already been assassinated, the security for Ted Kennedy was very strong. The good thing was that Kennedy loved the Secret Service and wanted us in close proximity to him at all times. He went out of his way to make sure we were fed and taken care of. I had never been around a protectee who treated us with that kind of respect and care.

We soon learned that his reputation with the ladies was in no way exaggerated. It was common knowledge that Senator Kennedy suffered with a degenerative back condition and consumed a variety of doctor prescribed medicine for the pain. No matter where we were spending the evening at our campaign stops, his staff always arranged for a "massage therapist" to visit Senator Kennedy and give him a "treatment" two or three times a week. Strangely, these therapists looked more like Playboy bunnies than anything else.

Knowing that Secret Service Agents were always outside his door or bedroom window, he always made sure the window was open so we could enjoy the sounds and or sights of his therapeutic treatments.

During his travels, he frequently visited many well known actresses and singers in Hollywood and Manhattan and overnighted (I do not feel at liberty to provide their names at this time).

If there was an event where food was being served, Kennedy always made sure that the agents working at that location were fed the same food everyone else was eating.

When the campaign ended and Senator Kennedy failed to get the Democratic nomination, we went to the Kennedy family compound at Hyannis Port, Massachusetts. There on the water is the beautiful Kennedy estate that his father, Joseph, built.

Even though our protective services for Senator Kennedy had concluded, he wanted to throw a going away party for his staff and protective detail. Caterers showed up and set up tents and tables. There were steaming pots of fresh lobsters, crab, oysters and clams, along with boiled potatoes and corn on the cob. There was also cold beer and champagne.

Senator Kennedy had a professional photographer on hand to take pictures with everybody present. There were about a dozen very attractive, female "physical therapists" on hand in case anyone needed a personal "treatment" that evening.

Say what you will about the man and his politics. I can honestly say I was never treated better by anyone I protected my whole career.

Kennedy

A Double Minded Man

-14-

THE REVEREND

A secret service agents career can often be defined by how many presidential election campaigns they have survived.

Even if you aren't at a point in your career where you are permanently assigned to a president or vice president for 3 to 5 years, you are going to be pulled away from your field investigative duties and assigned to a presidential candidate during the election cycles.

Obviously you had no idea as to who those candidates were going to be and when they would be given Secret Service protection. It had to do with their prominence and threat assessment as well as how much support they garnered.

A Double Minded Man

A new agent is always excited about participating in their first presidential campaign. All the travel, all the people, all the new places. All the new experiences. After about 30 days on the road, it all begins to run together and loses its luster quickly. I often set the telephone book on the nightstand in my hotel room to remind me the city I was in before going to sleep.

You can never let your guard down. You must always be looking; looking for that person who doesn't fit. That person who looks out of place or is not reacting like everybody else in the crowd. You are tired, you get to stand when other people are sitting. When they are eating you are standing.

Spectators are always making stupid remarks to you.

You still have to always be on guard, always ready to react

You're always on camera. Surrounded by the media who are recording your every move and word. You can't trust any of them. Anything they hear you say can be taken out of context. The media are not your friends. They are there to get a story and sensationalize it. If there is an assassination attempt they want to get every second

The Reverand

of it on film.

The candidates' staff are not your friends. It is a constant give and take with them. They don't care about security or the candidate safety. They care about exposing their candidate and his or her message to as many people as they can. The media, the staff, and the Secret Service all have a job to do. Unfortunately, their jobs all conflict with one another.

One of my most memorable campaigns occurred in 1988. I was assigned to the Reverend Jesse Jackson. The campaign slogan was "The Year of Jackson. The Rainbow Coalition."

This was not going to be an easy assignment.

It didn't take long to realize that Jackson's campaign was operating on a shoestring budget and his staff was made up of a bunch of amateur straphangers and White House wannabes.

The only thing impressive they had going for them was a strong Secret Service detail. Jesse Jackson's protective detail was made up of highly experienced agents. His threat assessment was very high and the Secret Service protected him to a higher degree because of his threat level. Most of the agents did not have a high regard for the Reverend Jackson as a person or his ideologies, but no one wanted anything to happen to him on their watch.

It soon became apparent, that Jackson's favorite speech venue was a capacity crowd at a Baptist church. If there was fried chicken before or after the speech, that was even better. The goal was to get everybody screaming in unison, "I am somebody."

If there was not fried chicken or food served, then you could expect that our motorcade would soon be stopping for a few buckets of Colonel Sanders' finest, followed by another stop at a roadside store to purchase moon pies.

A few minutes later, you could always count on the fact that chicken bones and moon pie wrappers would soon be exiting the windows of the candidates limousine and his staff vehicle and littering US Highways.

We traveled by air on a private, twin engine prop powered aircraft that was manufactured in the 1940s for the US Air Force and was now converted for civilian use. Although the pilots seemed capable, the aircraft did not. There was always a puddle of oil on the pavement underneath each engine when we arrived at the air-

The Reverend

plane.

On several occasions, the plane would lift off without a clear understanding of what its destination was. Sometimes we would take off with an understanding that we were going to a speaking event in Cleveland, Ohio and mid-air, the staff would decide to go to Des Moines, Iowa instead. You can imagine what a nightmare that was for an agent on the ground whose responsibility it was to secure our arrival spot, speaking site and have a motorcade in place when we arrived.

On more than one occasion we landed at an airfield and there was no one on the ground waiting for us. It was a campaign circus.

Because the Reverend Jackson spoke at so many Baptist churches, I got to hear some of the most amazing black choirs in the world. Needless to say a white, blue-eyed, blonde haired agent like myself did not exactly fit in a room full of black supporters. But it was all I could do to keep from clapping my hands and stomping my feet when those choirs were singing before and after Jackson's speech.

Of course we had the normal challenges with racially charged protesters. But our biggest problem was with members of the Black Muslim

Nation, who showed up at many of our events thinking they should provide their own form of security and protection to the Reverend Jackson. These guys were always immaculately dressed, armed and had no respect for official law enforcement.

The Reverand

A Double Minded Man

-15-

NEW ORDERS

In the Secret Service you are old at age 40. Very old at 45 and shouldn't be there at age 50.

If you are an active field or protection agent, the demands on you are physically as well as psychologically enormous. A 40-hr. work week is non-existent unless you are a desk agent. Days off may not occur for weeks at a time, depending on the investigative case you are working or the protection assignment you may have. Yet, you are always expected to perform at peak levels without error or lapses in judgment.

I had just turned 31. I was in the best physical condition of my life. I belonged to an unofficial, unauthorized club. We called ourselves the 300. It had nothing to do with how many members there were. It was all about how strong you were.

Membership required your ability to bench press at least 300 lbs., do one squat with 300 lbs. and dead lift 300 lbs. There were obviously no female members of the club. It was strictly a macho thing.

At 31, I was in the second year of my protection assignment in Washington, D.C.

I just wanted to do my minimum requirement of three years and then return to a nice field office on the West Coast. I had no intention of becoming a "beltway bandit," which is what many agents become after their first field office assignment. They are brought to Washington, D.C. to fulfill their protection duties, which may be three to five years. They then rotate into a headquarters division, such as training, intelligence or internal affairs. They get promoted, begin to drink in the bars with the supervisor decision-makers and begin to focus only on themselves, their careers and their next promotion. These agents just circle around inside the Washington, D.C. beltway, feathering their nests and never return to the field. I'm not saying that's wrong. It's just that more often than not they begin to have little regard for the agents in the 70+ field offices around the world and think the center of the universe is Washington, D.C. Don't get me wrong, I believe every American should spend some time in Washington, D.C. After all it is our great nation's Capital and one of the most amazing places in the world.

I enjoy history. Every opportunity I had, I took my family and explored every historical site we could find up and down the east coast.

The buildings, structures and monuments in D.C. symbolize power, strength, and our testament to the Christian roots and foundation that our nation was built upon. Unfortunately now when I think of Washington, D.C., adjectives like power, greed, corruption, ineptness and waste come to mind.

I was pulling a tour of duty with VPPD (Vice President Protection Division). The Vice President lives in a stately white mansion situated on a hill at the Naval Observatory compound. It was a great assignment because the compound is located in the mission and embassy district, about 5 miles from the White House and Capital hub of Washington, D.C. I was working the day shift.

In protection, you change shifts every two weeks. You barely get used to one shift when it is time to change again. I had just parked my personally owned vehicle in the compound and was walking towards the command post for the daily briefing by the shift commander, when another agent notified me that the boss wanted to talk to me. Those are usually words you do not want to hear. It usually means you are in trouble and are going to get your ass chewed out. That was my general assumption because I can never remember an occasion where I was notified that the boss wanted me to come to his office for a compliment.

I knocked on the SAIC's office door and was told to come in and have a seat. Sitting off to the side were two other agents that I didn't recognize. I surmised that they had something to do with training division as they were wearing black SWAT type uniforms and boots with their pant legs tucked inside. They looked stern and serious. The SAIC introduced me to them and then explained that the Secret Service had been authorized to develop several specialized teams. These teams would be removed from their normal assigned duties and would receive specialized training over the next few weeks and months. The purpose of these teams was to counter an attack against a secret service protectee. Two teams were going to be created initially.

I was told that among all of the agents in Washington, D.C., I had been selected to be on CAT team number one. CAT was an acronym for

"Counter Assault Team." I was told to report to the Beltsville, Maryland training facility, which was less than an hour away, the following morning at 8 a.m. I was less than thrilled. As previously stated, I just wanted to get this Washington, D.C. tour of duty over so I could get back into the field. I was concerned this might prolong the length of my Washington, D.C. stint. I was advised that the director of the Secret Service along with the full approval of the President had authorized the development of these special elite SWAT type teams. So whatever choice I might have thought I had in the matter had already been made for me.

The following day, I kissed my family goodbye in the morning at our suburban Washington, D.C. home. At the training facility in Beltsville, I learned that the two experimental CAT teams would be made up of four agents each. These four-man teams would train together and would function as a single unit. We were to receive specialized weapons and combat-type training from the agency, but also from other sources within the government as well as from private contractors.

The CAT team's mission was to identify and eliminate a life-threatening problem before it occurred. If a large scale attack against a Secret

Service protectee should occur, then this military style team would engage the attackers and either draw fire away from the protectee and or destroy the attackers.

As I previously mentioned, I was 31 and in the best physical condition of my life. I could not have imagined what the next 60 days would be like.

New Orders

A Double Minded Man

-16-

C.A.T.

The training was brutal, and 12 hour days were a common occurrence. We ran and ran some more. We crawled on our bellies in the dirt. We carried each other on our backs. We fired thousands and thousands of rounds of ammunition, from rifles, shotguns, hand guns and automatic weapons. Classroom instruction was kept to a minimum. You learn more when you're doing, not talking about doing.

After two weeks at Beltsville, the eight of us reported to an Army training facility nearby. There we encountered the US Army's Delta Force. Delta Force: the U.S. Army's 1st Special Operational Detachment used for hostage rescue and counterterrorism, as well as direct action and reconnaissance against high value targets. Under their tutelage we were brutalized and trained by the Army's best. Running and shooting, running and shooting, running some more and shooting some more. Raiding buildings. Firefights on aircraft, in the woods and in open fields. Combat scenarios against live opponents in every conceivable situation and physical area. Every day you were bruised, broken, and you bled.

Our team had a government issued van assigned to take us home and bring us back to the training facility each day. Each day the van brought me home, the sliding side door was opened and I was shoved out in front of the house. Most evenings I was too exhausted or in too much pain to walk without assistance, and I would crawl to the front door, or, if she saw me in time, was assisted by Mic, my wife. Every day she was horrified at my appearance and physical condition. She was not happy and wanted me out of this assignment.

Fortunately our children were too young to remember this time or these events. Mic helped me clean up and get dressed. I could see her looking at the cuts, scrapes and bruises covering my body. It was not a pretty site.

"Just one more day," I told her and myself, not realizing this was going to continue for three more weeks.

After dinner, I would collapse in bed and repeat the process the next day. Mic knew to not ask a lot of questions or burden me with family issues. She knew I couldn't drop out and I wouldn't quit.

In these situations, other people are counting on you. The respect of your teammates becomes the paramount objective. You can't let them down. As always, in the Secret Service, your family (if you have one) becomes secondary.

We simulated every kind of attack situation imaginable. City streets, motorcades, enclosed and open parking lots, on rooftops and airport terminals. In planes, trains and trucks, swamps, deserts and coastlines.

After Delta training, we returned to Beltsville for two weeks.

Cat Team 2 had lost a man, who broke his ankle jumping from a moving vehicle during a Delta training exercise. Cat Team 2 was taken out of training and we never saw them again.

The next two weeks consisted of training from private contractors. Hand to hand combat training against single and multiple attackers. Attackers with knives, swords, rocks and clubs. This training was provided by martial arts instructors and others who were considered to be the best in their field. It taught you how to physically disable or kill your opponent with your bare hands no matter what their size. You learn how to inflict the most amount of damage in the shortest period of time. This was some of the best training I ever received. It still comes in handy today from time to time. However, at this stage of my life I have painful areas on my body as a result of injuries I sustained from punches and kicks received during that training.

After that, we assumed we had survived the worst of it. However in a few days we found ourselves being delivered to the East Coast Navy SEAL training facility at Little Creek, Virginia, near Virginia Beach.

The United States Navy's Sea, Air and Land Teams, commonly known as the Navy SEALS, are the U.S. Navy's principal special operations force and a part of the Naval Special Warfare Command and United States Special Operations Command. One of the SEALS primary functions is to conduct small-unit maritime military operations which originate from, and return to a river, ocean, swamp, delta, or coastline. Seals can negotiate shallow water areas such as the Persian Gulf coastline, where large ships and submarines are limited due to depth. The Navy SEALS are trained to operate in all environments (Sea, Air, and Land) for which they are named. SEALS are also prepared to operate in a variety of climates, such as desert, arctic, and jungle.

I think that since the SEAL team instructors knew we were civilians, they thought we were soft. They decided to make the next two weeks a living hell and see how much abuse they could dish out. We were given our own private bunker. Every night, we were awakened by flash/bang bombs, yelling, screaming and cold water being thrown in our faces.

Although we did not scuba dive, we did a lot of underwater and ocean survival exercises in swimming pools. This included the infamous death capsule, where you were belted into a pod which then was released to slide into a swimming pool and turned upside down, in pitch dark. You were totally disoriented, blind, and holding your breath. The objective was to free yourself from the seat belts, open the capsule and figure out how to get to the surface of the water before you drowned. Since I'm here to tell the tale, I clearly survived, but I still have nightmares about not making it through that experience.

The training was mandatory, because years

before, during the Nixon administration, two Secret Service agents drowned when their helicopter, returning to San Clemente, California from offshore Catalina Island, went down in the ocean at night. Nixon had a beachfront house in San Clemente, which he used as his "Western White House."

Sniper training was our main objective for being at the Navy SEAL facility. SEAL team snipers are unquestionably the best in the world. Even though we had already qualified at 1000 yards at the Beltsville firearms range that had all been with stationary targets in ideal conditions. We now learned the skills and techniques of stealth, disguise, and camouflage as well as patience. We learned how wind, temperature, humidity, and elevation affect the trajectory of a bullet and how to compensate for those conditions.

Our final two days with the SEALS were devoted to ocean survival. Early one morning, wearing only swim trunks, we were loaded onto a Navy helicopter and flown several miles from shore. The helicopter then hovered about 30 or 40 feet above the water and we were told to jump. Two instructors jumped into the water with us. The helicopter then left the area and we were left treading water. The ocean water was approximately 60 degrees. After the initial shock of the cold water, my body began to adjust to the temperature. But within 15 minutes, I realized I was cold and beginning to shiver. The SEAL instructors taught us how to conserve energy and how to respond to a shark attack. We were in the ocean for 30 minutes before the helicopter returned. As the helicopter hovered above, a cable was lowered with a harness and one by one we were winched up into the helicopter.

After lunch, we were instructed to get dressed in business attire - suits, ties and dress shoes. We soon found ourselves in the same helicopter flying 30 or 40 feet over the same area of ocean water. The door was then opened and we were instructed to jump again into the ocean. At first we just sat in our seats in disbelief, thinking that the SEAL instructors were joking. They weren't.

One by one, we leapt into the cold ocean water. At first our clothing helped retain body heat, but we soon began to feel the devastating effects of the added weight of our clothing and the extra effort it took to keep our heads above water and stay afloat. Fortunately, the instructors were continually yelling at us and forcing us to keep fighting the ocean.

I can't begin to describe the relief I felt when

I saw the helicopter coming to retrieve us. I was the last one to be pulled from the ocean. By then I was losing the battle, and the instructors were having to keep me afloat.

As I was being winched into the air toward the helicopter, something happened that would affect me the rest of my life.

When I was approximately 10 feet from the floor of the helicopter, the winch suddenly stopped working and the cable's tension went slack. Within moments, I was free falling. I fell approximately 15 or 20 feet and then the cable suddenly jerked and stopped my fall. My arms and shoulders flew upward and my neck snapped backward violently. I felt a sharp pain in my neck and my body went completely limp. I could not feel my body from the neck down! I thought I was paralyzed. The cable hauled me the rest of the way up. It was a long, long 30 feet. After being loaded onto the chopper terrified and completely incapacitated, I slowly began to feel tingling and sensation return to my body. Eventually I told the instructors that I was OK, but I was worried, I knew that I wasn't. After being examined by one of the base Navy doctors, we both hoped I had just suffered some tendon strain and would be OK in a few days. He suggested I might want to wear a neck brace for a while.

C.A.T.

That was not going to happen. I was not going to be seen in a neck brace or let anyone know I was less than 100%. I was not going to get removed from this program the last day and let my teammates down after all we had been through together.

A Double Minded Man

-17-

SURGERY/RECOVERY

The next few weeks did bring healing to my body, but not completely. If I turned my head suddenly, I felt a sharp pain in my neck and would see stars. Also, I had a constant nervous twitch in my left tricep and only half the grip strength that I possessed previously. I could no longer bench press 300 pounds or even 200 at that point.

I went to see the White House physician. After examining me, he concluded that I probably had one or two ruptured discs in my neck which was putting pressure on my spinal column. He suggested I make an appointment with a neurologist and an orthopedic surgeon. Now I was really concerned.

I continued to train with my team. Depending

on the intelligence and threat assessment, CAT Team One now accompanied the President or Vice President on their foreign travels

I did not let my teammates or anyone else other than my wife know that I was having these physical challenges.

After meeting with a neurologist and orthopedic surgeon, I was scheduled for an MRI, because x-rays did not reveal a problem. Unfortunately, to no one's surprise the MRI revealed that I indeed had a ruptured disc between vertebrae C6 and C7 in my neck. It was considered serious and could in fact have caused paralysis. I was scheduled for surgery within days.

A lot of things run through your mind when facing a major surgery. Especially one where the doctor tells you it's too risky to enter your neck from the back and therefore will be operating from the front and entering at the base of your neck. The risk there according to the neurosurgeon and orthopedic surgeon is that the larynx, windpipe, voice box and esophagus all must be pushed out of the way to get to the spinal column.

The possible effect of doing that is one may have difficulty swallowing and or talking thereafter. But due to the severity of the ruptured disc and the possibility of paralysis, there was no question it needed to be fixed.

Before arriving at the hospital, I made sure my will was correct and the life insurance was paid and up to date. I tried to assure Mic that everything would be fine and there was nothing to worry about. But inside I was unsure. In fact I still had abrasions and bruises that weren't healed from the CAT training and now this.

How do you mentally prepare for a major surgery? I didn't know. Never been there or done that.

My process went like this: We were scheduled to report to the hospital at 8 a.m. Mic made arrangements with the neighbors to keep the children. At check-in, you are required to submit proof of insurance and fill out 7 pages of past and present medical and family history; then you wait for 45 minutes. This delay gives you plenty of time to observe the other poor souls in the waiting room and ponder the nature of their problem.

Finally you are called back where a nurse or someone wearing scrubs, takes your weight, blood pressure and pulse and tells you to strip and put on the hospital gown. The one that must be tied from behind. Fortunately Mic was still with me to tie the gown and take my clothes.

We said our good-byes and I told Mic how much I loved her and not to worry. Then I was alone - alone to think about my life.

We are all born with a birth date. Then there is the death date and what about that dash in between? What will it say about you? Will you make any lasting contribution? Will your great grand children even know your name? I thought about my great grandparents for a few moments and quickly realized I didn't know anything about them. Why? Did they do anything worth knowing about?

While deep in thought, there was finally a knock on the door and a doctor entered and introduced himself as the anesthesiologist. After a bunch of medical questions he left and then I was prepped for surgery. An I.V. was inserted on top of my right hand and taped in place. A heart rate monitor was clipped to my finger and suction cups with wires leading to a machine were attached.

Then I was wheeled into the operating room. It was brightly illuminated and cold. Why was

Surgery/Recovery

it so cold, I wondered? Four or five people were waiting. All wearing surgical scrubs, face masks and rubber gloves.

One of the men in the room approached. "I'm Dr. Cross; I'll be doing your surgery today. We are going to take good care of you today. Take a couple deep breaths; we are going to put you to sleep now."

I could feel my heart pounding and I silently prayed that all would turn out well and that I would make a full recovery.

And then it was silent and dark. Nothing. No out of body experience. Just nothing! Is that what death is like I wondered afterwards. Just nothing?

I have since talked to numerous anesthesiologists about making people unconscious. They all say there is continuous brain activity but the amount varies from person to person. Some people dream and remember while others have no memory awareness.

When I was awakened after the surgery, I immediately felt relief. The pain in my neck, shoulder and arms was gone. The surgeon was concerned about my vocal chords and voice since the surgery was performed through the front of my neck. He had removed the ruptured disc and replaced it with a piece of bone that was harvested from my pelvis, which in time would eventually grow together with vertebrae C6 and C7, fusing them solidly together. My voice did not suffer long term effects and returned to normal in a couple of weeks.

After the surgery, while I was still at the hospital, I received a visitor. It was my SAIC (Special Agent in Charge). At first I was flattered that he would visit me. But after a few minutes of small talk, he got down to business, he suggested that I would not be able to meet the requirements of the job in the future and stated he might be able to get me transferred to some other government position. A desk job of some type (pushing paper from the inbox to the outbox), or he could even recommend some form of disability.

I was determined to prove him wrong. I determined that I would make a full recovery. I was required to wear a neck brace 24/7 to stabilize my neck. I had no neck discomfort, but the pain in my pelvis, the site from which they had taken that piece of bone was intense. I had to practically learn to walk again with that leg. My hospital visit only lasted 4 days. I was then sent home with a walker dragging my left leg. I was

Surgery/Recovery

unprepared for the pain created by removing the left top side of my pelvic bone - and the subsequent disability. I was told I would need weeks of physical therapy. I knew the neck would take a few weeks for the vertebrae and donor bone to grow together, but I was determined to speed up the healing process of my leg.

Several times a day over the next few weeks Mic would stabilize me as I forced myself to walk the length of the cul-de-sac in front of our house. There seemed to be no progress for days, but eventually feeling, strength and control began to return.

The orthopedic surgeon told me later that muscle and ligaments had been detached from the pelvis and reattached after the bone was removed. There is also no risk of rejection if your own bone is used in a fusion.

Over the next 6 weeks I recovered. Every opportunity I had, I went to the gym or went running. Eventually I regained strength and speed.

I was not ready to rejoin the 300 club, but was ready to return to some form of work. I had read every book in the house to my children at least 10 times!

Mic and I had also engaged in numerous conversations about leaving the Secret Service, finishing law school and getting a normal job with a nice air conditioned office. The thought of sitting at a desk pushing paper was appalling to me after the adventures I had experienced the previous five years.

Besides; I had to prove to my SAIC, my teammates and most of all myself, that I could still do the job.

I went to my SAIC and requested I be allowed to return to my team. He was reluctant but I convinced him to allow me to go to Beltsville for a day to prove that I was capable of performing my duties alongside my teammates.

After two days of rigorous testing of my abilities with firearms, hand-to-hand combat, and physical performance, I got the green light. I had done it. Once again I was lean, mean, hard and strong. I was confident in my physical abilities, equipment and my teammates. I knew I could react instinctively and with deadly force to any threatening situation that might come my way in the future.

CAT Team One was glad to have me back; they had been grounded as a result of my inju-

Surgery/Recovery

ries. We were once more a team. I was now officially and forever a member of the first Secret Service CAT Team. CAT Team Number One.

Every time we were included in a Presidential or Vice Presidential trip, we silently prayed that something bad would happen so we could utilize our hard-won skills. Much like a fighter pilot or navy seal, most inwardly crave a battle to fight after all of their training and preparation.

To my knowledge, only CAT 1 and CAT 2 received the kind of extensive field training that we had. Other teams did follow, but it was decided by the supervisors that training to that extent was not necessary in the civilian world.

As a CAT Team member, if you weren't on standby or actually working an event, you were training or fulfilling your normal duties. Trained warriors without a war can become disgruntled. The Secret Service did not know what to do with CAT Team One. We no longer looked at the world through the same rose-colored glasses as our fellow agents in their pin-striped suits and penny loafers. We were warriors.

A Double Minded Man

LIFE IS CHEAP

I was first exposed to the low value that is placed on life by some governments, especially in foreign countries, while traveling abroad as part of a protective security detail with former President George H. W. Bush. This point was driven home in an unforgettable way. As you may remember, President Bush was the former U.S. Ambassador to China prior to being Vice President and President of the United States. During his terms in office, he traveled there frequently to foster trade and improve relations between the United States and China.

While providing security on one of those trips, our entourage was traveling by motorcade from Beijing to a small village to view farming practices, or so we were told. I don't know why we were really making that trip and it didn't matter. It was a need to know basis. I also didn't care. I was there along with the other S.S. Agents to provide security for the President of the United States and didn't give a damn about the Chinese.

The motorcade consisted of approximately 18 vehicles. First in line was a pilot car consisting of a S.S. agent and a Chinese intelligence officer counterpart. They ran the route approximately five minutes ahead of the main motorcade to make sure the route was clear. Their job was also to make sure all the security requirements along the route had been implemented by the Chinese Military, (making sure police and military were properly posted). Entry-sections were blocked and there would be no surprises. The Secret Service does not like surprises. As you can imagine, everything is carefully planned days in advance and every possible problem in a plan put in place, just in case. No matter what happens there is a proper response and everybody knows what to do.

Next came two armored Chinese Army vehicles each carrying six heavily armed Chinese soldiers. They had been screened and handpicked. This was followed by the Secret Service provided vehicles flown to location for that moment by the U.S. Air Force on a C-5 transport. On a foreign visit like this there is always two of everything - a spare aircraft, helicopter and limousine.

When traveling abroad across the ocean, the Navy even positions ships every few hundred miles in case a rescue is needed. Satellites in space are even repositioned for communication purposes.

Next was the spare limousine. Identical to the main limo except it doesn't carry the President. The President is moved from one vehicle to the other so the public does not know what car he is riding in. But it is mainly there in case there is a mechanical problem with the primary limousine. It is usually filled to maximum capacity with presidential staffers or high level members of the host country. They are only driven by highly trained S.S. agents. If something should happen to the presidential limo, any occupants in the spare limo are removed and the President is placed in the spare.

Following the presidential limo is the follow up vehicle which is usually a specially equipped and fortified SUV designed to carry the working shift, which in public, provides the inner circle of security around POTUS. This vehicle is occupied by a Secret Service agent driver; the shift leader in the front seat, two or three agents in the second seat and a tail agent in the rear facing the back holding an automatic weapon.

This is usually followed by a number of vehicles containing approved traveling staff, military attaché, medical doctor, traveling press, more local media, and depending on the location, more military and local police and even an ambulance.

Naturally, the movement of this motorcade interferes with everything going on for miles as traffic, trains, planes and people are diverted to other areas.

It should also be noted that POTUS could be located anywhere in the motorcade, even an unmarked or military vehicle or a secondary motorcade. This is all determined by the advance team threat assessment before POTUS even touches down in the country. The threat assessment also determines how big and how heavily armed the traveling security package will be.

On this particular morning, I occupied the tail position in the back of the follow up black SUV. All the windows are always down for obvious reasons.

The air-quality around all major cities in China is horrendous, due to the coal that is burned

Life is Cheap

to produce power and electricity. Most Chinese burn it to heat their homes also. The sun looks like a dull orange ball through the brackish charcoal gray haze that is everywhere.

The last place in China I wanted to be at that moment was in the rear of that follow up. All the exhaust fumes from the Suburban as well as the preceding vehicles were being pulled into the back draft created by the boxy SUV. This, combined with the acidic black coal dust that filled the air and covered everything in China, was quickly turning the inside of my collar and shirt cuffs on my freshly laundered white shirt to black. I hated to think what it was doing to my lungs. So I wasn't real happy that morning.

Our motorcade had only traveled about 13 km from the landing zone. The landing zone was at a military base on the outskirts of Beijing and we had to travel through an agricultural area with a few hills, steep terrain and narrow roads. We had just entered the hill country, when suddenly our motorcade came to a abrupt halt. This wasn't good. A motorcade should never stop until it reaches its destination or unless there is a serious problem.

The agents immediately flung open the heavily armored doors, jumped from the follow up vehicle and surrounded POTUS's limo with guns in the ready position. We could see nothing, but there was loud shouting in Chinese ahead of us. We could also see that several Chinese military members were also out of their vehicles. Our shift leader was talking on his sleeve microphone trying to find out what was going on.

I was calm, but ready. My finger was gently touching the trigger guard of the cocked Uzi submachine gun.

Suddenly the shouting in Chinese turned angry. Then three shots from a Chinese AK 47 rang out followed by five or six more. My heart was pounding. I was on full alert. We thought we were coming under attack but were soon notified on the radio earpieces that everything was OK and we could proceed. The motorcade began to creep forward and we continued to run alongside the armored limousine at the ready position. One hundred yards ahead we observed the threat that had been neutralized by the Chinese military.

A peasant.

Yes, a peasant had come down a mountain trail walking his donkey that was towing a cart loaded with firewood. The peasant and his cart had come onto the narrow roadway after the lookout

Life is Cheap

pilot car had already passed. The peasant was blocking the roadway and had tried to maneuver his donkey and cart up a steep embankment so the motorcade could pass. However, the heavily laden cart had broken free and rolled backwards into the side of a Chinese military vehicle.

The military then executed the Chinese peasant and his donkey and pushed their cart and bodies off the side of the road.

A Double Minded Man

-19-

NSS

One cold February day I was told by my SAIC, that I had a private assignment and was to meet with a man named Vance at 7 p.m. at a nearby Roy Rogers Restaurant a few blocks from the White House. I was told to tell nobody what I was doing or where I was going. I was to listen carefully and consider his offer.

As I entered the restaurant, I saw a man wearing a dark top coat and hat sitting in a booth drinking coffee alone. I had been told to ask if he had an umbrella I could borrow. That was the code to identify. Vance looked to me to be Egyptian. He had sharp facial features and cold black eyes. Vance talked to me philosophically, about freedom and liberty, good and bad, right and wrong, the American way of life and what it takes to keep our enemies at bay. All the things he talked about and described I believed in already. He then asked me if I would be willing to fight to defend this country and protect its citizens and reminded me of the oath I had taken when I became a Secret Service Agent.

He also wanted to know what I thought and how I felt about taking the life of another human being. At first I didn't know what to say. It felt like I was in a movie scene. I looked around to see who else was in the restaurant. A dozen other customers were there, but no one to be concerned about. Then I saw him. A clean cut man with a short beard sipping coffee in the far corner. Although looking away, he was watching us, using the window for reflection.

After a brief silence I responded that I had crossed that bridge in my mind a long time ago. I said, "I would have no problem killing someone that needed to be killed."

After a few more minutes Vance said, "I will be in touch," and got up and left. The man in the corner also left.

I never saw Burton Vance again. Thus began a parallel "career" with a secret agency within the government that I only knew as NSS.

NSS

My only contact with the NSS was through Burton Vance. In fact, I never knew what NSS even stood for. So I made up things myself, such as national secret society; no stupid stuff; nothing said society; or need to save society.

I was instructed to never ever discuss or mention anything I ever did for the NSS with anybody. This included other CAT Team members.

Sometimes I would be gone from the Secret Service without explanation as were other members of CAT Team One. When we were next together, and looked into each other's eyes, we knew. We knew that unspeakable things had occurred. And we also knew that because of what we had done, our small contribution, that our American way of life was safe for another day.

In the beginning, requests from Burton Vance were infrequent and unexpected, maybe two or three times in a year. After I left D.C. and transferred back to the field they became more frequent, especially during President Reagan's final year in office. It was as if there were scores to settle.

I always received my instructions via a special ringtone on my telephone. If I was unable to answer, a mechanical voice left a five digit numerical code. I then entered that code into the phone along with an assigned five digit code that I retained. I was then notified that I had a new target and that a package with all the details photographs and information I needed for my assignment was in a post office box awaiting my retrieval. If I did not retrieve the package and respond within 48 hours, the package was removed and the assignment was withdrawn from me. Sometimes the assignments took me to other countries and sometimes I stayed inside US borders.

I remember my first assignment. I couldn't wait to get to the post office box and retrieve the package. I didn't know what to expect, but I didn't expect to see what I saw. There was detailed information about when and where the target would be available. The how was up to me. I guess I was expecting to see pictures of somebody who looked like a terrorist or hardened criminal mug shot. Instead, there were photographs of a neatly groomed caucasian man who was 31 years old. There were pictures of him with what I guessed to be family members – wife, children.

Not what I was expecting. I was given detailed information of this man's schedule and itinerary for the next five days. I thought there would be more information about the evil things the target had done, information that would justify the extermination.

The decision makers at NSS or above had determined that this individual was apparently a threat to America or Americans and should be eliminated within the next five days. I did not want to know any more details about this person's personal life.

Requests like this were also infrequent during President Bush's term of office until the last six months of his four year term and then several different assignments came my way.

A field agent's investigative duties are frequently interrupted by protective assignments, locally, nationally and globally.

So when an NSS request came in, it was easy to pad it to look like just another Secret Service travel away from home assignment to your fellow agents and your family. Even your supervisors did not know the true nature of your whereabouts.

Sometimes they are a welcome change of pace depending on the location. But often, they are a major disruption of your field investigations. After you have walked away from your caseload for a week or two, all your leads are now cold and your information is no longer current.

The best part of my assignments was there were no reports to be filed. No affidavits created. No concern about defense lawyers, Miranda rights or any form of due process. No travel vouchers to submit. No United Nation rules or restrictions. No nothing.

I simply notified Vance that the deed was done at the earliest possible opportunity. I was always asked the same two questions. Any collateral damage? Any loose ends?

Never did I hear, "Are you okay?" Or, "How are you?" Or, "Do you need a therapist or a shrink or some form of counseling?" Nor, "Are you suffering from Post Traumatic Stress Syndrome?"

My response to the questions was always NO. To which the reply was always, "Good and good day."

The important thing was that within a few days, a sum of tax-free money always appeared in my personal, private, for-business-only bank account. I never knew what the amount would be until it appeared. It was as if different targets were assigned different values - much like a video game.

I always worked alone. Only I was responsible for my safety. Only I knew how I was going to carry out the request. And only I would have to suffer the consequences if things went wrong. I would assume all the risk. The government would officially deny any involvement and claim I acted alone or on my own. If captured, I might be rescued but I couldn't count on it. I'm sure I was considered expendable and not of high value. I was to only carry out orders and did not possess any sensitive information that my government would be concerned about. I'm sure my only value was to carry out the assignment. If I couldn't do it, I guess somebody else would.

You could confide in no one. Who would believe you anyway?

During the years of President Clinton's first term, 1992 to 1996, there was no contact with Burton Vance or NSS. My career with the U.S.S.S. was coming to a close and I was looking at my future. A life without the Secret Service. A completely new life. A life that didn't involve guns and violence and lies to my family and people who knew me.

USSS and NSS seemed like a movie. A story or novel I was reading. Not my life.

I was looking for an exit. A way out. An opportunity to just be a normal guy; a normal husband, father and member of society. I was tired of the double life. Life wasn't simple anymore. I had seen too much waste, corruption, bribes and double standards. So much spin. Eventually you don't know what the truth is.

There is what the media reports, what politicians say, what the official report states and of course what really happened, which nobody seems to care about. Nothing black and white, just shades of gray.

I was becoming more cynical and disillusioned with each passing day.

I was hoping there would be light at the end of the tunnel.

NSS

A Double Minded Man

-20-

THE NEWSY

Although the Secret Service, White House staff and national press have a close personal relationship, our goals and objectives are vastly different. At times we just tolerate each other.

But sometimes they step over the line.

One such occasion occurred during President Ronald Reagan's second term. We were preparing for an overseas trip. Air Force One was being readied at Andrews Air Force Base, Maryland.

Another agent and I were on the tarmac with a member of the Air Force One crew. Our job was to check the manifest and make sure no one boarded Air Force One without proper identification and their name on the manifest.

Suddenly a well-known news reporter (we called these people "newsies"), who a few months before had been promoted to the position of anchorman on the evening news for one of the major networks, approached our location carrying a briefcase and large suitcase.

He dropped his bags at our feet and said "Make sure these get on the plane."

We tried to explain to him that he was required to stay with his luggage as we could not have unsecured, unattended luggage sitting on the tarmac. The newsy then proceeded to tell us how important and famous he was. He announced that he was leaving his luggage and would return after he made a phone call and demanded we put his luggage on the plane

My coworker and the Air Force One flight attendant all agreed this newsy needed a lesson in manners and respect. My coworker pulled out his knife and within moments the name tags and security clearance stickers on the luggage disappeared.

I radioed the command post and notified them that we had a couple of suspicious packages with no identification lying on the tarmac near Air Force One. I requested that they send an

The Newsy

EOD (explosive ordinance) team to our location immediately as Rawhide (Reagan's code name) was already in route via Marina One (Reagan's helicopter).

Within moments, the bomb team arrived with their armor plated trailer. They carefully grabbed the abandoned luggage with long extension poles and placed them in the trailer. The bomb team then transported the luggage to the far end of the runway.

A couple minutes later we heard the "poof poof" sound of distant explosive charges and saw two clouds of gray white smoke.

We high-fived each other and were still laughing when Marine One landed with Rawhide.

A few minutes after we had become airborne and reached our cruising altitude, the hotshot newsy came into our seating area asking everyone where his briefcase had been placed.

To him we all look alike so he didn't know who to direct that question to. We all denied any knowledge.

To my knowledge that news anchor was always polite and courteous to the Secret Service after that.

The Newsy

A Double Minded Man

-21-

THREAT FROM WINNEMUCCA

The US Secret Service has the daunting task of protecting questionably the most powerful person on the planet. The scope and infrastructure required to accomplish that task far exceeds what the average person would conceive. Without going into the physical mechanics of that, at this time, let me say that the Agency must keep tabs on approximately 40,000 people around the country, who are considered a possible threat to the protectees.

For example, when the President or Vice President or a foreign leader equivalent to our President plans to visit a city, weeks prior to that visit, agents from the intelligence division begin assessing the threat level. They must determine if any known persons in those geographic areas should be put under surveillance or detained who might have an interest in assassinating our protectee.

For example, if you are discussing politics with a friend in a bar and are overheard making a comment such as, "I hate President so and so and if I had a chance, I would put a bullet in his head." An innocuous statement like that reported to the Secret Service by a bystander would get you a visit from two agents, whose job is to determine if you are a serious threat to the President. If you meant what you said, have the means or ability to carry out such a threat, you could be prosecuted. If you were considered to not be a threat, you still have a case number and a file from that day forward and would always be considered a person of interest.

Based on the personal encounter with the subject making the threat as well as interviews with friends, associates and family members, a determination would have to be made as to their ability to carry out the threat if they wanted to, such as: Do they have a firearm? Are they mobile? Do they have transportation? Do they have the physical skill and ability, etc.? It's a judgmental, gut feeling, opinion call. And you better be right when your name goes on the assessment.

Of the many field assessments I made in my

career, one of them always stands out above the rest. I received a referral from the White House when I was assigned to the Reno, Nevada district. It was a rambling, threatening letter from somebody who obviously hated the President and his administration. There was no doubt that the author of the letter wanted the President and his family dead. The letter only contained a P.O. Box return address in Winnemucca, Nevada.

After contacting a postal inspector to determine who the P.O. Box was registered to, we had a suspect name and physical address in the high desert of northern Nevada. I grabbed an agent named Steve Diangelo, who we called Guido and we were soon traveling east on Interstate 80.

I liked Guido. He was 31 years old, married to an overweight Italian gal from New York, who had provided him with three sons. Guido was a good field agent but he was a Jersey boy from the big city and did not fit into the west. It was obvious to everyone, that Guido was in Reno to punch his ticket to fulfill his small office career development requirement. He had not done his tour of duty in Washington, D.C. yet so he was not tainted or corrupted by that environment. Many good field agents eventually go to D.C. to do their protection time and end up bouncing around from one headquarters office to another, ass kissing their way over to the next promotion and lose contact with the hands on work that actually goes on in the field offices.

After arriving in the small mining community of Winnemucca, Nevada, we soon found ourselves driving for miles on a rutted out dirt road in the middle of open range land covered with sagebrush.

Eventually, there was no doubt we had arrived at the location we were looking for. In the middle of nowhere was a 10 acre plot of land surrounded by an 8 ft chain-link fence with razor wire on top. The driveway was secured with a chain and padlock gate.

In the center of the fenced off property stood a single wide mobile home, that was approximately 40 ft. long. Parked next to it was a dirty Dodge Ram pickup painted army green. We honked our horn several times and were greeted by two barking black Rottweilers. I eventually got out of the vehicle and began to holler for Mr. Mathews.

Within a few minutes, a tall thin man wearing only a pair of jeans opened the door and stepped out onto the landing. Guido said, "Holy shit, he's got a rifle."

Threat From Winnemucca

We ran to the back of the car for cover as Mr. Mathews pointed the rifle into the air and fired off a round. Matthews said, "Get the hell off my property."

"Federal agents," I yelled. "We are just here to talk. Put the gun down." In the trunk of our vehicle, we carried a shotgun and an Uzi 9 mm submachine gun. However, we exited the vehicle so rapidly, that we now found ourselves standing by the trunk of the vehicle with the keys in the ignition.

I yelled again, "Police, we just want to ask you a few questions. Put the gun down."
Matthews sat the rifle down and leaned it against the trailer. "Unlock the gate and get your dogs," I said. Mathews whistled and the dogs ran back to the trailer. It's not locked he said.

I motioned for Guido to open the gate. As I pulled the car forward Mathews yelled, "Close it!" Guido got back in the car and said, "Holy shit, holy shit, I wasn't expecting all of that." My heart was pounding but I chuckled and said, "You never know."

As we proceeded toward Mathews and the trailer, we began to notice the landscape was covered with piles of dirt and large craters about

6 to 10 ft. in diameter. Very strange. Next to the trailer was a 10 ft. TV satellite dish with a happy face painted on it.

We exited the vehicle and identified ourselves as Secret Service agents. I told Guido to grab Mathew's rifle, which turned out to be a 410 gauge shotgun. I asked Mathews if he had any other weapons and he said, "No."

We then invited ourselves in. It was far worse than I had imagined.

The trailer was filthy. It smelled of urine and rotting food. The sink was full of dirty dishes and furnishings consisted of a dirty worn recliner next to a table with a reading lamp on it and an old television. Old boxes, books, newspapers, and pornographic magazines were piled everywhere. You literally had to turn sideways to maneuver through the trash in the trailer. It was unbearable. We were wearing suits. Way over dressed for the occasion and our surroundings.

I suggested we go outside and talk

As we walked around the property, I showed Mathews the threatening letter and he confirmed that he had written it. Mathews hated the government and politicians in general. He was a hermit, who believed politicians in Washington were ruining the country.

When asked about the dirt piles and craters covering his property, he explained that the Mormons had been visiting him and were trying to get him to donate his property and possessions to the church.

Mathews said he had taken dynamite and exploded it all over his land, thinking if he did that the Mormons wouldn't want or try to take his property.

We eventually ended up sitting in the government vehicle and questioned Mathews for about an hour. We found most of Mathew's answers ridiculous and humorous.

I asked Mathews what he spent most of his day doing and he replied, "I just sit in my trailer and jack-off most of the time." I glanced into the back seat at Guido. He was making a masturbation gesture with both of his hands. We couldn't take it anymore. We both began to chuckle and eventually it turned into uncontrollable laughter. Even Mathews began to laugh. We were helpless. I was laughing so hard I couldn't keep my eyes open and tears were running down my cheeks. Mathews could have taken our guns and killed us. We were laughing so hard we were helpless.

We concluded that Mathews, although not of sound mind, was not a realistic threat to the President or other protectees and did not need to be put on any kind of a watch list. Mathews never ventured away from Winnemucca, had no other weapons and did not have the financial means to travel and carry out a death threat. Guido and I continued to laugh about our experience with Mathews all the way back to Reno.

Threat From Winnemucca

A Double Minded Man

-22-

CAROL - OFFICE MANAGER

The Reno field office was run by the office manager Carol Johnson. She was the receptionist, the administrator, in charge of inventory control, operated the radio and dispatcher. She was like a mother to the agents who work there. She could probably conduct interviews and investigations if permitted. She screened all the calls and the in person walk-ins to the office. Everybody had to go through her first.

Carol was a buffer. She covered for you and always had your back. Everybody loved Carol.

Carol was in her mid 50s, attractive, with short brown hair. She had obviously been a beauty in her younger years. She was a widow and lived alone. She always took a personal interest in every agent, their spouse, children and personal life. Carol had lived in Reno many years and seemed to know everything about the area and had connections everywhere. We all loved Carol and when she was on leave, the office ceased to function.

My office door was the closest to her work area.

My long time friend, Tommy Jackson, from Oklahoma City, happened to be coming through Reno. We met for lunch in one of the casino restaurants and decided to create some drama for Carol.

I radioed the office and verified that no one was there except Carol. I then notified her that I was bringing in a suspect and would be there in approximately 15 minutes.

Before entering the office, I handcuffed Tommy. Tommy's role was to play the part of a resistant, belligerent, foulmouthed suspect. I shoved Tommy through the door and he went into his act. Tommy began yelling, "You'll pay for this," and swore at me.

He looked at Carol and said, "What are you looking at bitch," as he kicked her desk. Carol's reaction was everything I hoped it would be. Her

Carol - Office Manager

mouth flew open and her eyes were wide. She was stunned. I slammed Tommy into a chair by my desk as he was struggling to free himself from my grasp. I slammed my office door closed, which Tommy took as his cue to really start performing. He went into a tirade about how he was going to kill me, my wife and kids.

We followed that verbal exchange with some physical banging, punching, smacking and fighting noises.

Carol was aghast. She ran out of the office down the hall to the other end of the building where the U.S. Customs office was, yelling, "Help, agent needs assistance."

With that, I quickly removed the handcuffs from Tommy, opened the office door and sat down at my desk. Tommy relaxed in a chair, put his hands behind his head, leaned back and propped his feet up on my desk as we waited for the cavalry to arrive. Within moments, two U.S. Customs Officers burst through the doorway followed by Carol.

I said, "What seems to be the problem," as Carol peeked into the doorway. She was still in a state of shock.

Tommy and I began to grin. Carol shouted, "You assholes," and walked back into her office. I apologized to the customs officers, who enjoyed our little prank. I kept trying to apologize to Carol but couldn't do so with a straight face and would always begin to laugh.

It took lunch and about a week before Carol was able to laugh about the incident along with everybody else in the Federal Building.

I seldom see my old friend Tommy. But when I do, we still talk about that incident and enjoy a good laugh together.

I wouldn't be surprised if Carol Johnson was still sitting at her desk in the Reno field office.

Carol - Office Manager

A Double Minded Man

-23-

FORMER PRESIDENT FORD

Reno, Nevada was my third official government duty station. Although I loved living in Reno with the Sierra Nevada mountains, snow skiing and Lake Tahoe and the beauty of the Nevada high desert, it definitely had some drawbacks.

Reno is a smaller version of Las Vegas with its gambling, organized crime, prostitution and all of the serendipities that it attracts. Most of the people who commit crimes and cause trouble in Reno are from California. The biggest problem with Reno, like Las Vegas, is that it is a 24 hour town that never stops. After four years I was burnt out and exhausted.

I was offered a promotion, which involved a transfer to former President Ford's detail. Being assigned to a former president's protective detail is not a sought after position if you are at all ambitious. You are more of a glorified valet and taxi service. Any good investigative field agent is bored to death most of the time. Like all protective details, there are three shifts working round-the-clock. On a former president detail most of your time is spent standing around being bored, wishing the protectee would go somewhere or do something.

Although I was not looking forward to the assignment, I knew I couldn't stay in Reno indefinitely and if I was going to transfer again, I might as well take the promotion. I was also tired of the grind in Reno and needed a break.

One of the beneficial prerequisites was that I knew how to snow ski. Just like if you were assigned to President Reagan, you needed to have equestrian skills.

Fortunately, President Gerald and Betty Ford were still active at this stage of their life. Betty Ford liked to shop around the Palm Springs area near their home in Rancho Mirage on the Thunderbird Golf Course. She also liked to attend concerts, get her hair and nails done and look after the affairs at the Betty Ford Center. She also attended a weekly Alcoholics Anonymous meeting. Gerald Ford swam daily, golfed regularly and hosted a couple charity golf tournaments every year which were attended by several Hollywood celebrities. They were also frequent guests of Bob Hope and Andy Williams who lived nearby.

Like most former presidents, Gerald Ford also earned money as a public speaker and was on several fortune 500 company boards of directors. He traveled monthly for meetings in Chicago, Minneapolis and New York.

They also spent the winter holidays at their Colorado Mountain home in Beavercreek, just west of Vail.

When things warmed up in the desert, Beavercreek became their main residence for about three months during summer.

This meant that the agents assigned to him also resided part of the year in Vail, Colorado and part of the year in the Palm Springs area. It could have been a lot worse.

So it was a great life for a couple of years, living like the rich and famous on a government salary.

A Double Minded Man

The Ford residence in Rancho Mirage was also situated next-door to another of Firestone's many residences. The Secret Service occupied a small guest home next to the Ford's. It was surrounded by a 10 ft. concrete wall with one electric gate providing in and out access. Secret Service controlled the gate access. The property was situated on the Thunderbird Golf Course and backed up to the 13th Fairway. It was surrounded by all varieties of citrus trees. I acquired a taste for grapefruit and ate two or three of them every day.

Without notice or green fees, President Ford frequently pulled his golf cart out of the garage and played holes 13 through 18. Daily dress was golf casual but we were required to keep a business suit in our locker. We also frequently rented tuxedos for formal evening events.

President Ford never carried cash. Every time we were at something that necessitated a tip, President Ford always fumbled around like he was looking for money and would then turn to me (the shift supervisor) and say Glenn can you get this, I will repay you later. He never did. He owes me about $200.

President Ford smoked a pipe. Although I do not smoke, I always enjoyed the aroma of his

Former President Ford

pipe tobacco which permeated his clothes and filled his office.

He also had not possessed a driver's license in years and had no need for one as he was driven by Secret Service everywhere he went. So, every chance he had he got behind the wheel of his golf cart. On more than one occasion, he got it stuck in sand traps and even turned it over in a ditch.

He went to the barber shop every other week. I always wondered why he never had a single gray hair.

His favorite swearword was "God dammit." If we were ever delayed in traffic, or at the airport, or things weren't going the way he thought they should, I can still hear him shouting, "God dammit! Who's responsible for this?"

I enjoyed my time with President and Mrs. Ford, but after two years I was ready to move on.

I think the only reason former Presidents are afforded protection for a few years after they leave office is because the U.S. Government does not want to deal with a possible embarrassing situation, such as a former President of the United States being kidnapped and held for ransom.

A Double Minded Man

-24-

NICKNAMES

Reputations are established early and difficult to change once established. Likewise nicknames get attached to agents as a result of a response to an activity or situation in which they are involved in. Those names are also subject to change during an agent's career.

During my first tour of duty in Los Angeles, I acquired my name. I recently ran into an old colleague I hadn't seen in at least a dozen years and he called me by my acquired nickname.

My partner and I had recently arrested a suspect for conspiracy, electronic fraud, assaulting a federal agent and resisting arrest. When originally confronted, he had run and then fought violently as we were apprehending him. He had made bail, but failed to show up for his court appearance. A fugitive warrant had been issued for his arrest.

Some federal agencies rely on the U.S. Marshals to hunt down and arrest their fugitives. The Secret Service does not. Larger field offices have their own fugitive squad and find and arrest their own fugitives.

My partner and I got a tip that our fugitive was now working at a construction site near the Los Angeles airport. Upon arrival, we saw a huge apartment complex was being framed. We located the foreman and after showing him photographs, he confirmed he did have an employee matching that description and radioed for him to come to the office.

When our suspect arrived and recognized my partner and me, he immediately turned and ran. My partner gave chase, but I ran toward the employee parking area, thinking he would try to make it to his vehicle. I was right. I tackled him from the side and we slammed into the ground. A struggle ensued. The suspect was still wearing his carpenter belt. He was trying to stab me with a nail extractor.

As we were wrestling on the ground, I was able to grab his framing hammer which had fall-

Nicknames

en out of his belt. I swung the hammer hard and slammed it into his right shin bone, breaking it. He began to cuss and scream.

The fight was over.

As my partner handcuffed our fugitive, he commented that I was still gripping the hammer. That event earned me the label "Hammer" from that day forward.

The defense attorney also filed a complaint against me of using "excessive force" against his client and that went into my employment file.

A Double Minded Man

-25-

LONG BEACH

Secret Service Academy Firearms Training and monthly re-qualifying is something every agent must do, but hopes to never utilize.

The training you received in the 10 week U.S. Secret Service Academy teaches you to only shoot your weapon to stop the assailant. "Stop" being a vague term, can mean anything from injury to the point the assailant is unable to function, to actually killing the perpetrator.

But in reality, we were trained that in close range firing situations, whenever possible, you always fired three rounds to neutralize your opponent. The first two rounds were always fired in rapid succession at the body mass, which is the largest target and area where the vital organs are held. Then immediately execute the kill shot, which is aimed at the head. So the instruction may be to "stop" the assailant. The actual training exercises that were performed over and over and were ingrained into our memory and response mechanism consisted of two body and one head shot. This is what a Secret Service Agent will instinctively do if placed in a life or death combative situation with a firearm.

That valuable training first came in real handy in Long Beach, California. At the time, I was assigned to the Los Angeles Field Office (LAFO). LAFO is a great training ground to find out who the real field agents are and who the posers are. I'm sure every company or organization has its posers; people who passed the academic, physical and interview process. They went through orientation training and probation, but still aren't worth a damn if something goes down and don't know how to respond in a life or death situation. You certainly don't want those people covering your back.

Government agencies at all levels are infected with these kinds of people, thanks to affirmative action, quotas and policymakers, who have never done what they are requiring others to do. And worse, they are establishing the procedures and guidelines as to how things should be done. It's like a chicken telling an eagle how to fly, and then setting limitations on how much it can flap its wings and how high and where it can soar.

LAFO is a nonstop grind where the 40 hr. work week is nonexistent. Where the criminal activity never stops or even lets up. A place where cases have to be prioritized and small time criminals are overlooked if the dollar damage is under $100,000, because there are so many multi-million dollar problems to deal with. It's a place to pay your dues and get the hell out; where posers are readily identified and shunned by the doers.

A LAFO Agent has had to deal with more shit in 4 years than an agent in Charleston, South Carolina would have to deal with in a 20 year career.

It's like comparing a Los Angeles Police officer to a Show Low, AZ cop that has no crime or criminals to deal with. Yet, both wear a uniform and carry the same equipment. But the LAPD Officer probably has to draw his gun everyday and the SLPD officer may never have a need to draw his weapon.

It was my first tour of duty in LAFO and I was not happy to be there. I had already paid my dues (or so I thought) having already served in San Francisco, Washington, D.C., Reno and Palm Springs. I had put in a request to be sent to Sacramento, California, close to where I grew up, where I could finish out my 20 year career and be forgotten. I had just finished a three year assignment in Riverside County and submitted my transfer request for Sacramento. Sacramento was not meant to be and Los Angeles always needed more agents, so the decision makers denied my request and I received transfer orders to Los Angeles.

I soon found myself residing in Orange County for my family's sake and commuting each way to the LAFO. That little drive took a mere 70 minutes at 3 a.m. or three hours on a rainy day.

I was in charge of the fraud/financial crimes squad. An understaffed group of 25 of the most selfless, dedicated, Los Angeles hardened men and women the agency had ever employed.

The posers made sure they weren't assigned to this squad, because the work was unending.

We even had a bunk room so agents could crash for a few hours when they were exhausted before going back to work. We definitely did not want guys to go home and waste time with their families. God only knows how a family and a home life could interfere with you staying on top of your case load.

One of my guys, by the name of Danny Diaz, had been probing into a group of gang bangers operating out of Long Beach.

Danny was from a family that had emigrated legally from Mexico before he was born. He was rough and bilingual. He kept his head shaved and maintained a black fu-man-chu mustache, which grew to the bottom of his jaw. He also had a tattoo of a hand giving you the finger on the back of his head. Danny was very scary looking. However, when he was not working the streets, he was a gentle soft spoken polite individual.

Danny loved working the streets of L.A. County. It was his home turf. He grew up in the badlands of Compton and fought his way through life. He actually had a graduate degree in chemical engineering. Danny was living proof that you can't judge a book by its cover.

Danny was rarely selected for temporary protection assignment because he did not fit the image the Secret Service wanted to put on camera next to a head of state. Danny was happy with that. But if you put him in a suit, shaved his face and let his hair grow out a few inches, he was one good looking Mexican.

We affectionately referred to Danny as "the butcher." Many agents carried some type of knife, but Danny kept a meat cleaver on his lower back. He had worked part-time as a butcher, putting himself through college in his previous life.

The Los Angeles Mexican gang bangers were involved in everything: robbery, guns, counterfeit ID, murder for hire, drugs and turf wars. Now they had moved into credit card fraud. One of the gang members had a girlfriend, who worked on the inside operations division of Wells Fargo. She had obtained a ream of credit card name and number information measuring about 12 inches thick. This computer paper contained the personal data of over 1 million customers. Wells Fargo had not even made a public announcement yet.

We also knew these guys were total "badasses," heavily armed with automatic weapons and would not be brought in with a smile and a "pretty please."

Danny had been working this case for weeks and had negotiated the purchase of some of these Wells Fargo documents. We had gathered evidence, obtained the necessary warrants and conducted liaison with counterparts at the Long Beach Police Department.

We were ready to drop the hammer, or should I say meat cleaver. Danny, I and two other senior agents in our squad went over every detail and planned the raid. We pulled a dozen members of our squad together and briefed everybody and went over assignments at 7 p.m. At 8 p.m., the meeting was over. Everyone had their assignments and was dismissed with instructions to report to the staging area in Long Beach at 4 a.m.

In a case like this, which is going to involve numerous suspects who will resist arrest if given the opportunity, surprise and deadly force is a must. I believe the term used by the Department of Defense during the first Gulf War and "Operation Desert Storm" was "shock and awe." It was Danny's case, so Danny requested the amount of manpower and equipment that he thought was needed. My job was to not second guess Danny, but to verify everything he requested, oversee the operation, and make sure he got what he wanted.

We decided to make our move at 4 a.m. Most crooks are asleep, passed out or unconscious at that time. They sure aren't getting up to an alarm and getting ready for work. The target site was a rundown two-story, 10 unit apartment complex in the Chicano district of Northeast Long Beach.

Our target was apartment number nine on the second floor. By installing pole cameras on utility poles around the complex, we had been able to conduct continuous surveillance for the past 48 hours. We knew there were at least four people in unit nine and two Pit Bulls. I hate Pit Bulls.

The gratifying aspect of Secret Service cases is that you are not responding to some violent life threatening event in progress, like uniformed police do daily. In our fieldwork, everything is after the fact. You hold all the cards and you can do things on your terms and on your schedule. The safety of your teammates is the highest priority.

I was worried about the damn dogs more than anything else. Did I tell you I hate Pit Bulls? The only reason someone would own a Pit Bull is for offense or defense. They are not pets.

At 4 a.m. our team was in a strip mall parking lot three blocks from our target apartment. Also present were the Long Beach Detectives and four black and white units. After a quick 20 minute briefing by Danny, to confirm everyone knew their position and role, we moved in unison to the apartment complex.

At precisely 4:30 a.m. we were in position. A new moon was just setting so it was pitch black except for the occasional porch and street light. The morning marine layer was heavy and wet making visibility difficult.

I was carrying my weapon of choice during these scenarios, a short barreled Remington 12 gauge shotgun with a folding stock, loaded with five rounds of 00 buckshot. This means every time you squeeze the trigger, 8 round lead balls come out of the barrel towards your intended target. I also carried my trusty 40 caliber Glock in my belt and a 38 caliber Smith and Wesson 2-inch on my ankle for emergencies. So far I have never been in that kind of emergency and prayed it wasn't going to be now.

At precisely 4:38 a.m. the raid began. Immediately you heard the muffled kush kush sound as the percussion grenades were fired through the front and back windows of unit nine. Following the sound of breaking glass came the blinding flash and ear bleeding bang as the grenades did their job. The ram at the front door took two swings to dislodge all the deadbolts. This was valuable time lost and my second clue after the barking pit bulls that this was not going to be a piece of cake.

I had taken up a position at the bottom of the stairs, gripping the cold steel of my shotgun. I waited nervously.

Suddenly all hell broke loose. The sound of gunfire and the popping of automatic weapons filled the air. There was screaming, hollering, cussing and then another exchange of gunfire that seemed to last forever. The door of unit three beneath unit nine, next to the stairwell, flung open. I was startled. Instantly, in the fog covered blackness of the door opening there was a muzzle flash two times in rapid succession, immediately followed by the sharp crack of two pistol shots.

I instinctively squeezed the trigger of my 12 gauge and felt myself punched backwards and knew it wasn't from the recoil of the shotgun. I had been shot, but the assailant was silent and there was just darkness in the doorway. I automatically pumped another round into the chamber and was glad I did. No sooner had I leveled the shotgun at the door again when out came a snarling Pit Bull. Without hesitation, I blasted the bitch back into the black hole it came out of.

Long Beach

Upstairs a woman was screaming and I could hear Danny's unmistakable voice with his Mexican accent yelling, "Shut the fuck up!" He liked to say that a lot in these situations.

I then became aware that two other agents were at my side, asking me if I was okay. I truly didn't know.

After the dust settled we had three gang bangers shot. Two critically wounded. Two pit bulls dead. Danny had been hit. One round grazed his thigh and another round struck him in the stomach but it was stopped by body armor. I had also been shot once in the right rib cage. Again, thank God for body armor. But it still hurt like hell, cracked a rib and made a bruise 6 inches across. I was careful to conceal this incident from Mic.

Within moments, the whole neighborhood was in an uproar. Police and ambulance sirens were wailing and the media parasites were on the scene.

But we saved Wells Fargo's butt and the public was not made aware that one million people's personal records were compromised.

A Double Minded Man

-26-

THE OLD PUEBLO

Tucson, Arizona, AKA The Old Pueblo, was a pleasant change from the grind of Los Angeles. When the opening became available, I marched into the Los Angeles SAIC's office. I knew the SAIC was on an upward career path and was well-connected in Washington, D.C.

I had carefully rehearsed my speech and effectively laid out all of my prior Secret Service work experience. I explained why I was the best candidate in the Secret Service to take over the position of RAIC in Tucson. Even though the SAIC did not owe me anything, I had done a decent job and had never given him any reason to doubt my abilities or performance.

I don't think there was a lot of competition for the position. Tucson is a remote isolated outpost with only a handful of agents assigned there. Most agents in Tucson want to operate under the radar. It is not someplace to go if you are trying to climb the Secret Service success ladder. I did not know anything about the demographics of Tucson, but I believed it had to be a better place to live and raise a family than Los Angeles County

The Tucson office covers a huge geographic area including all of southern Arizona from California to Texas and the state of Sonora, Mexico. The RAIC of Tucson answered to the SAIC in Phoenix Arizona.

Upon reporting for duty in Tucson, I was given a brand-new government issued Oldsmobile, a nice private corner office with my name tag and title on my fake mahogany desk. I also had my own private covered parking space.

After getting my desk and office in order, I was requested to attend an office meeting in Phoenix. I knew several of the field agents in Phoenix, but was not acquainted with the supervisors there, especially the SAIC.

I had been advised that the SAIC had previously been assigned to the D.C. Internal Affairs division, had a drinking problem and had therefore fallen from grace and sent to Phoenix to finish his career. SAIC Spangler fit the mental image I had of him. He was approximately 50 years old, somewhat short by agent standards with thinning gray hair. He appeared to be in poor physical condition and definitely had the reddish complexion of many hard drinking men.

SAIC Spangler complimented me on my "stellar" Secret Service career and then began to explain the poor performance of the Tucson district and the agents who worked there. He stated he expected me to change all of that for the better. He made it very clear that my job was to make him look good and if I did that we would have no problems in Arizona.

One of my main priorities in Tucson was to establish relationships and trust with other law-enforcement officials in southern Arizona and Sonora, Mexico. I wanted to let them know that there was "a new sheriff in town" and that they could rely on me. I also wanted to be able to rely on them to share information and criminal Intel and to cooperate in joint investigations. I made sure to personally visit all of the sheriffs, police chiefs and U.S. Federal Agency SAIC/RAICs in my district on a monthly basis. This was no small feat.

I also attempted to establish relations with the police and federal officials in the state of Sonora, Mexico, but soon found, as I suspected, that there was much corruption and there was nobody I could completely trust. However American dollars can get you a lot of information from corrupt police and Federales in Mexico. Every visit to Mexico always included what amounted to hundreds of dollars in bribery money exchanging hands.

Sometimes you find yourself playing God. Deciding who gets locked up and who gets a pass. Who comes in vertical or horizontal. My small team of agents in Arizona had been investigating and arresting some small low-level criminals, mostly Mexican, who were in possession of false IDs, driver's licenses, passports, Social Security cards and birth certificates as well as counterfeit money.

We had traced the source back to a Mexican national known as Orlando.

Orlando was one of the worst criminals I had ever dealt with. He was wanted by the DEA, ATF, FBI, and ICE. Orlando was into drugs, guns, counterfeiting, human trafficking and anything that created revenue. His file was thick and full of bloody pictures of his victims that he

The Old Pueblo

had tortured and mutilated. Some were children. American prisons were too good for a man like Orlando.

Through an informant, we had received a tip that Orlando was living with his family on the outskirts of Douglas, Arizona. It's a border town near the Mexico port of entry Agua Prieta, Sonora, Mexico.

After weeks of surveillance, we had verified his existence, but had concluded there was no way to take down Orlando without a violent confrontation.

A decade prior, I would have welcomed a violent confrontation. But now I was older and wiser. Broken noses, cracked ribs, three knee surgeries, fused neck vertebrae and a reconstructed wrist had made me wiser.

Plus, I had a wife and children I wanted to grow old with and there was the safety of my teammates I had to think about. But inside, I really believed prison was too good for a man like Orlando and wanted this man to die slowly and painfully, to give him the same kind of justice that he had administered to his victims.

Orlando's residence was surrounded by a cement block wall. Two bodyguards with automatic weapons were often present and two or three Rottweilers roamed the property. I hate Rottweilers.

From surveillance video, it was obvious that Orlando loved his wife and three children and they loved him. It was very contradictory to see him express such love and affection to his family, knowing the vicious, cold torture and violence he administered to others.

I knew we could call in the tactical teams and overwhelm Orlando with force, but that would put my team at great risk and the paper work would be horrendous. Not to mention the Monday morning quarterbacking and dealing with the media.

No, as much as I wanted to take Orlando into the Sonoran Desert and torture him to death, I knew there had to be a better way. I had recently been reading a classic book by Dale Carnegie, "How to Win Friends and Influence People", trying to improve my people skills. I also had a psychology degree. I reviewed Carnegie's chapter on respect. He points out how important that is to a man and that most criminals don't see themselves as such and feel they can justify their behavior. So I decided to take a different approach.

The Old Pueblo

I kept surveillance and sniper teams around his residence. I obtained the phone number to his residence and decided to give him a call. At first he didn't believe who I was when I identified myself, so I told him to hang up and find the office number of the nearest US Secret Service. Call it and ask for me.

It was at least 10 minutes before the call came in. After listening to him rant about what would happen to any agents who came near his property, I calmly explained that his residence was already surrounded and under surveillance right now. I explained that I already had arrest and search warrants in my possession and that the US Grand Jury had handed down a 19 count indictment and that we were going to arrest him. I also told him that if he tried to leave his residence, we would shoot him dead and justify it as self-defense.

After Orlando stopped cursing and telling me I was bluffing, I asked him to step outside and look at his HumVee, which was parked nearby. I then radioed one of the snipers to put a bullet into the windshield. Orlando cursed at me some more, but that got his attention.

I explained that he had two choices: Choice 1: We would come get him with teargas and guns blazing. We would kill his dogs and bodyguards and that his wife and kids would probably be harmed. We would then drag him across the dirt in front of his family and put him in a empty van and drive him to a remote location in the desert. And when we were finished with him he would tell us everything he had ever done.

Choice 2: He could enjoy the rest of the day with his wife. Play with his children. Pet his dogs, put his affairs in order, make love to his wife and we would then escort him to my office at 9 a.m. the following morning. I said we would have coffee and donuts available and treat him with respect. Either way, he was going down. It was his choice how. Orlando chose option 2.

The better part of me wanted this man to die in a hail of police bullets, but it was more important that my men went home safely to their families.

From that day forward, I changed my arrest procedures whenever possible.

The Old Pueblo

A Double Minded Man

-27-

FALSELY ACCUSED

After one year of effort in the Tucson area, performance had greatly improved. Arrest and conviction numbers had quadrupled and cases investigated had tripled. I had become SAIC Spangler's golden boy and he was delighted. He was able to include Tucson's statistics with Phoenix, which made his district look very good to the Washington, D.C. bean counters. In fact he was hoping to get reinstated to a position in Washington, D.C. eventually.

For the next 18 months, I could do no wrong. I only saw Spangler about four times a year when I attended quarterly district meetings in Phoenix. He never bothered to come to Tucson and would send the Phoenix ASAIC (Assistant Special Agent in Charge) to Tucson every three months to fulfill a headquarters requirement. I disliked this man because he had never done any real agent field work, had always been a pencil pusher and Monday morning quarterback, who questioned everything real agents did. He also had a reputation of throwing you under the bus for anything.

I made it a point to be in the field every time I had advance warning that the ASAIC was coming for a visit. I believed it was best to minimize my contact with a man like that, especially when I need to constantly be on guard with anything I said or did in his presence that might later be used against me. I would soon learn how correct my opinion of him was.

Every five years agents from Secret Service Internal Affairs come to the various field offices and conduct internal investigations. They make sure operational procedures are being followed and the offices are being managed according to procedural policy and that all inventory, evidence and accounting procedures are being followed. They also interview every agent assigned to the office to see if there are any problems that need to be addressed. These inspections usually take between one and three weeks depending on the size of the field office. Tucson's inspection received glowing comments and accolades from the inspectors. However, SAIC Spangler, received criticism because the Tucson office with 25% of the manpower had higher statistics than the Phoenix office did.

So instead of making SAIC Spangler "look good" I had made him look bad. From that day forward, I could do no right as Spangler felt threatened by me and in spite of what I said, believed I was trying to get his position. Every report or document submitted to Phoenix was returned because something was supposedly incorrect. I was no longer the golden boy from Los Angeles and everything I did was considered improper by Spangler from that day forward. I did not know it until months later that Spangler had accused me of violating all kinds of Secret Service policies and had requested internal affairs to launch an investigation into my present and past behavior in the Tucson district.

Spangler also had ASAIC Baronowski, who was an accountant in his previous life, looking at mileage logs, activity reports and informant payments, trying to find discrepancies that could be brought to the attention of the Internal Affairs inspectors. Spangler wanted to bring me down.

I first became aware of this Internal Affairs investigation after I'd noticed unusual cars parked in my neighborhood from time to time. Since I lived on acreage in the desert approximately 20 miles from the field office, it is hard to put a car in my neighborhood without it being noticed. It also became obvious that I was being followed every time I was in my government owned vehicle driving anywhere during duty hours. Since it is a violation to use your official government assigned vehicle for anything other than official duties, many agents have fallen victim to that violation, if nothing else can be found on them.

One evening I stopped at a strip club to check in with a paid informant that I had arrested about a year prior for being in possession of counterfeit currency. I arranged to have the charges against her dropped as she was more valuable to me as a paid informant outside of jail.

I noticed that I had been followed throughout the day and was being followed by two males in an obvious rental car. As I parked my vehicle and casually entered the strip club I noticed in the reflection of the darkened building windows where my followers were parked.

I'm sure they felt confident they now had the evidence to accuse me of some government violation: A government supervisor after hours in a government car on unofficial/personal business, at a strip club. What more could they hope for?

Falsely Accused

After entering the strip club, I went straight to the back of the bar, through the dressing room and out the back door of the building. I then circled around another building and came up behind the vehicle and the two men who had been tailing me. The man in the passenger seat was busy taking photographs of my government vehicle parked in front of the strip club.

It was a warm Arizona evening and their windows were rolled down. I pressed the muzzle of my 40 caliber Glock against the man's right temple and told him and the driver "make one move and you're a dead man." I then demanded that they show me identification. To my surprise, I found out they were Secret Service inspectors from D.C. Internal Affairs. They were there at the request of SAIC Spangler after he had made the false accusations about me and had requested this internal investigation.

The next day, I drove to Phoenix and confronted SAIC Spangler and ASAIC Baronowski. He accused me of embezzling government informant funds, using my government vehicle for personal business, using government ammunition for personal use, as well as falsifying government activity reports. He also accused me of making sexually inappropriate remarks to the female employees in my office and racial comments to minorities under my supervision. He even accused me of assaulting two fellow SS Agents. All of this, of course, was lies and fabrication on his behalf in an attempt to have me fired or transferred - to get rid of me.

"This is bullshit and you know it." Give me one example," I demanded.

"We don't have to give you anything," ASA-IC Baronowski said. He had been sitting quietly in the corner with a smirk on his face until now. I fought back the urge to grab that little ass-kisser by the throat and bash his face in. He went on to say, "I have provided the Inspectors with all the evidence. You are probably going to be arrested."

"What do you have to say for yourself? Now's your opportunity to come clean," said SAIC Spangler. It was obvious he was trying to provoke me and was recording this conversation. I took a deep breath and slowly exhaled. "You can kiss my ass. I don't have to tell you anything." I said as I stood up and exited. Several eavesdroppers outside the room gave me a thumbs-up as I left the office.

It was obvious that things were going to change for me. Two weeks later I was ordered to report to the Internal Affairs office in Washington, D.C.

I was escorted into an interrogation room. Very similar to what you see on TV cop shows - plain walls with the exception of a framed picture of POTUS. A table with four chairs, one entrance and exit door and a two-way mirror on the wall.

Two inspectors walked in dressed in dark, Washington, D.C. style suits and placed two large files on the table. These were the same two agents I had confronted outside the strip club in Tucson. One Inspector offered me coffee or water. The other remained silent. "I suppose this is going to be good cop, bad cop." I said. To my surprise, they both smiled and chuckled. "No, we wouldn't do that to you. Just relax, we are on your side."

I didn't believe that for a second. I apologized for threatening to kill them in Tucson. One responded, "Had I been in your shoes, I would have done the same."

One file contained all of my assignments transfers and accolades since my hiring date. The other file contained all the accusations and supporting documentation from SAIC Spangler and ASAIC Baronowski, as well as the Inspectors findings and interviews.

They began by giving me a copy of the affidavits submitted by Spangler and Baronowski, laying out the accusations and vague dates and places of occurrence. They then read them aloud and retrieved my copy. I was becoming nauseous and angry as I listened, but knew I had to remain calm and confident.

"Is there anything in these affidavits you would like to comment on?" "Yes," I said, as I reached for the recorder and moved it closer to me. "Let the record show that I said, everything SAIC Spangler and ASAIC Baronowski have accused me of is bullshit and lies, fabrications and misrepresentations and if you guys conducted any kind of legitimate investigation and examined the evidence you would have come to the same conclusion. I would also be willing to submit to a polygraph if Spangler and Baronowski will."

The Inspectors looked at one another and then asked "Anything else?" "I believe that covers my defense. I did not do any of the things they accused me of and you should know that by now, if you did your job. I'm sure you have already reached your conclusions."

Falsely Accused

With that they stood up, grabbed the files. Before exiting one of the inspectors turned and said, "We did do our job and have reached our conclusions."

I sat alone for the next 10 minutes staring at the clock on the wall and occasionally glancing at the two-way mirror wondering who was behind the glass. I replayed the previous 20 minutes over in my mind: the accusations. Should I have responded differently? Asked for mercy? This whole thing was such a crock. The Secret Service should be glad to have a guy like me and proud of the contributions and service I have rendered up to now. I just wanted to finish out my 20 year career in peace and then go have a life. Suddenly the door opened and a smiling face I recognized entered the room. I found myself shaking hands with an agent from the past. I had first met and become acquainted with Bernie Wilson years earlier when the Reverend Jessie Jackson ran for president. Bernie, was a black, well respected agent that had been assigned to be the detail supervisor, responsible for the Jackson's protective detail. We had spent many months on the road together until Jessie Jackson dropped out of the presidential race and the detail was dissolved. Bernie was a large, muscular man with a big smile and loved to laugh. With the same last name, Bernie and I often joked that we were brothers from another mother.

I hadn't followed his career path and was unaware until now that he was D.A.D (Deputy Assistant Director) over inspection. He reported only to the Director of the Secret Service. After exchanging pleasantries about families and career tracks, we got down to business. "Glenn," he began, "I have been brought up to speed on this case. Let me say first of all, the Inspectors have informed me that they have been unable to find any evidence supporting the accusations Spangler and Baronowski have made about you. In fact, after reviewing your performance in that office, I think you should receive an award."

"By the way, I wish I could have been there when you pressed your Glock to the side of Joe's temple at that strip club." He laughed.

"Whatever," I said. "So does that mean I can go back to doing my job without interference and harassment from Phoenix?" "Yes and no," Bernie replied. "Yes you can go back to doing your job, but no, it won't be in Tucson. We need to transfer you out of there."

"You've got to be kidding. Are you serious? You just said your investigators proved I had done nothing wrong and now you're telling me

Falsely Accused

I need to transfer. Transfer Spangler and Baronowski. Those pathetic, insecure bastards are the ones that should be transferred or forced to retire. I'm sure you wouldn't have to look far to find plenty of dirt on them. In fact, I would be glad to go back and build a truthful case on both of them."

"Calm down Glenn, sit down." I hadn't realized I had stood up and was shouting. "Let's get real. You and I both know how things work. Both Spangler and Baronowski out rank you and rank has it's privileges. Plus you know Spangler was a former Inspector and he and the Director go way back. So right or wrong, what they want carries more weight than what you want." I started to protest, but Bernie held up his hand.

"Let me finish," he said.

"There's a position available at the Washington Field Office that would be perfect for a guy like you. It would be a higher pay grade and would be a promotion. It's a pretty soft position and you would also receive a cost of living adjustment for living in D.C., which would mean a bigger retirement check someday. I'm confident I could make that happen, so what do you say?"

"Are you done," I asked? Bernie nodded.

"Look Bernie, I appreciate what you are trying to do here, but you and I both know this is wrong. That file of mine in front of you proves that I have more than paid my dues and up to now have had an unblemished career. I have served in big offices, medium size offices and small offices. I've done protection time here in D.C. I've moved my family six times already. I've built a home in Tucson and my kids are now in high school."

"I'm not uprooting the family again. I've only got a year and a half to finish my 20 and then I'm resigning my commission," I firmly stated.

"Glenn, I sympathize with you. I know it's not fair and you are getting a raw deal, but under the circumstances you can't stay in Arizona."

"This is so wrong," I protested and pounded the desk with my fist.

"The decision has already been made. It's over my head. Take the transfer. Finish your time! You'll be money ahead in the long run."

"And if I refuse?" "Then you resign," said Bernie. "Is there somewhere else I can go?" "Like where?" "Like Hawaii," I said. Thinking maybe I could sell that to my family. Bernie grinned. "Give me a minute," he said and left the room.

A few minutes later Bernie returned. The grin was no longer on his face. "You can go back to L.A. or take D.C. That's it." "I moved to Tucson to get my family out of L.A," I said. The thought of going back there was killing me. How could I go back home and tell my wife and kids we were moving back to L.A., let alone D.C. after promising them we were done moving? I felt sick to my stomach. I put my elbows on the table and held my head in my hands. Bernie was silent. Finally I said, "I'll go to L.A., but I'm not moving my family or accepting a transfer." "Wow," Bernie said. "Are you sure you want to do that? You'll receive no expense money. No cost of living adjustment, no travel compensation, nothing!" "Yea, I'm sure."

"OK," he sighed, "let me see if I can sell this." He was only gone a minute or two. My mind was whirling with thoughts of how this was going to impact my life. My family's life.

Bernie entered and said, "OK, you got it. I hope you know what you are doing." Of course they said yes. Spangler and Baronowski get what they want and the Secret Service doesn't have to spend any of their budget to relocate me and my family. Right then I began to think about how I could make Spangler and Baronowski pay for causing this.

Bernie said, "Go home and get your affairs in order. You've got 60 days to report to L.A." He held out his hand, "I'm really sorry about all this Glenn. I know you got a raw deal. I did all I could, but I couldn't make this go away." "I understand," I said. "No hard feelings towards you. It was good to see you again."

As I sat in silence on the plane ride back to Arizona, I replayed my Secret Service career up to this point in my head. This was no way to finish. I didn't deserve this. Everything in my life would now have to change. This was not how I planned to finish my career. This was all Spangler and Baronowski's fault. I don't know how, but some way or another I would make them pay.

At that moment, I believe a piece of my heart turned black.

Falsely Accused

A Double Minded Man

-28-

LOS ANGELES AGAIN

Unfortunately, a false reputation preceded me to Los Angeles. SAIC Spangler had informed the SAIC in Los Angeles that I was a troublemaker and that I had done all of the things they had accused me of doing. A new SAIC had replaced the one I had left in Los Angeles three years prior. Also, many of the agents had transferred and been replaced by new agents I did not know. I came in with a black cloud over me. The new SAIC informed me that he was not proud to have me in his office based on what he had been told and that he would be watching me closely.

I was assigned to the Los Angeles counterfeiting and financial crimes squad. The hardest working most dangerous squad in the office. I was given a number of cases involving several known members of the Russian Mafia. Some of the most dangerous criminals in the country, who compared to Russian laws and punishment think our system is a joke. They call U.S. prisons "Country Clubs."

We felt it best to leave my wife and kids in their home in Tucson and I commuted to and from Los Angeles whenever I had a day or two off. It was 400 plus miles each way. I had to use my own personal vehicle to make the drive. Since I had refused to officially transfer, I had to find a place to rent in Los Angeles.

Through an old California State Police contact, I heard about an old lady who lived in the Rampart District, Koreatown of Los Angeles. She lived in an upstairs apartment and liked to rent one of her bedrooms to police officers as it made her feel safe.

Gladys turned out to be a spunky old lady of 90 years. She believed cayenne pepper was the secret to health and longevity and created and consumed her own gel capsules of cayenne pepper each day. Before long, Gladys had me swallowing cayenne capsules. I expected my stomach to be on fire, but there were no unhealthy side effects. Gladys kept a bowl of pepper capsules prominently displayed near the kitchen sink, so I could have easy access.

She was a widow who had a daughter that lived in the area but did not speak well about her.

I agreed to pay her $90 a month for a bedroom and use of the bathroom. I was also responsible for my own meals and washing any dishes or utensils I utilize.

Gladys was a joy, full of Los Angeles history and stories. She had worked as a cleaning woman for many of the wealthy residents of Beverly Hills most of her adult life.

Because of work, I would go days at a time without seeing her awake. She was always pleased when we could visit and watch television for a few hours together. I don't recall sleeping in her apartment a single night without hearing police sirens, gunshots and seeing LAPD helicopter search lights shining into my bedroom window.

I was actually sad and teary-eyed when I said goodbye to Gladys and went home to my family for the last time. Gladys died about six months later.

A Double Minded Man

-29-

THE RUSSIANS

The last time I had been in Los Angeles, I was a respected squad leader. Now, I was the guy who had screwed up in Tucson and had been sent back to Los Angeles as punishment. I was the guy that other agents whispered about and pointed to behind my back. I had to prove myself all over again.

In most areas of the United States, Secret Service field agents have a pile of felony cases to investigate, determine who is responsible and locate and arrest the person(s) responsible. Case closed, next. Most of the time you work alone or with a local detective counterpart that has a mutual interest in the case. If the investigation is big and complex with lots of suspects, then a team of agents may be assigned to the case as well as a member of the U.S. Attorney's office. Two days after I returned to the Los Angeles Field Office, I was called into the SAIC's office. The SAIC introduced me to Agent Ernie Cologne and stated he was going to be my partner. Ernie looked to be about 25, wore reading glasses on top of his head, like other people wear sun glasses indoors. He was thin, about 6'2. His skin looked like he hadn't been in the sun in years.

I started to protest that I didn't need or want a partner, but decided to keep calm and act thankful. "Yes Sir!" I said, "Thank You." It was obvious that Ernie was being assigned to watch my every move and my methods of operation and report back to the SAIC.

As it turned out, Ernie was actually 37, divorced, spoke Spanish and French, because his mother was French and his father was Spanish. He had served in Miami for a number of years and worked in the Caribbean and South America. He had also spent 5 years in Europe assigned to the Paris field office. However he looked like a nerd and I quickly summarized, accurately, that he had spent most of his Secret Service career sitting behind a desk in front of a screen working as an analyst. The man had no scars on his pale white face or hands.

Every scar has a story behind it. Usually

embellished and exaggerated, but still a story. It's hard to trust a man with no scars. It usually means very little life experience and no physical capabilities. I like people with scars. Not people who sit in temperature controlled offices and second guess and analyze what people with scars have done.

Among the case load assigned to me was a thick file containing information about a group of Russians, who operated out of an ocean front home in Malibu, a self storage facility in the San Fernando Valley and a loading dock in San Pedro. Apparently these Russians imported counterfeit U.S. currency that was being printed with the approval and backing of the Iraq Government. In fact, these counterfeit notes were being printed with intaglio presses, which are very expensive and used by the U.S. Treasury.

Most small time counterfeiters acquire an offset style printing press, green and black ink, paper stock and after a few days of trial and error, can produce a Federal Reserve note that is passable in most bars.

But these Russians/Iraq notes were high quality and had been showing up in Southern California by the tens of thousands for a couple of years. The main case agent, Ernie Perez, had been transferred to a new duty station and now the files had been assigned to me.

I'm certain no one else in the squad wanted to inherit this investigation and I couldn't blame them. It's so much easier to start with something from the beginning and take it to it's conclusion. All you have to work with is the reports in a file and there's so much more in an investigators head and personal notes that never gets put on paper. Things like instinct, hunches, gut feeling and informant information. Sometimes you even have to break a few laws to accomplish what needs to get done.

The last thing anyone needs in an investigation like this is to have some unmarked, desk agent analyst as a "partner" whose main job is to report your behavior to the SAIC.

However, the more I read the case file (which took about 3 days), I became obsessed with it. I contacted the case agent, who was now on VPPD (Vice Presidential Protection Division) in Washington, D.C. As I suspected, the former case agent Perez, knew much more than he had put on paper. In fact he had identified most of the major players and even discussed the case several times with a member of the U.S. Attorney's Office in L.A., but didn't have enough evidence to take the case to the U.S. Grand Jury for indictments. It's so much better to run with a case that the Grand Jury has issued indictments on. You don't have to worry about probable cause or criminal rights. All that has been dealt with. You just get to focus on the search, seizures and arrests.

As I mentioned earlier, Russian criminals are a different breed. Our justice system, with all the rights of the accused, is a joke to them. If you make an arrest, you can't "flip" them or threaten them into cooperating or helping you. That's a death sentence from their fellow Russians, which they fear more than any American jurisprudence or justice system.

Our U.S. prisons are expense paid country clubs to them with better living conditions than they had outside of prison in the former Soviet Union.

You have to catch them in the act with the evidence in their possession. I think some law enforcement officers do not pursue these criminals because they fear retribution against themselves or their families. I didn't get the impression from the former case agent that fear of retribution had any impact on his investigation. He simply ran out of time and was transferred before he could bring this matter to a conclusion. In fact he expressed sincere empathy for the 100's of small mom & pop businesses that had been victims of these high quality counterfeit Federal Reserve notes.

If you are in possession of illegal contraband ie: counterfeit money, you are committing a federal felony and anything that contained the counterfeit money can be seized by the government unless you can show that you are the victim. In that case the money is confiscated and you are provided with a receipt, which you can use as a deduction on your IRS tax form. Wonderful, huh? However, if you knowingly pass the counterfeit money to somebody else, because you don't want to eat the loss, you are really screwed.

After following up on leads and talking to numerous victims and Los Angeles area law enforcement detectives and conferring with Agent Perez, I concluded the Russian leader, who presided over this groups activities was Ivan Federoff. He occupied the residence in Malibu. His "go to man" that oversaw their criminals enterprises was Markoff Lukin.

Both Federoff and Lukin had served together in the Soviet Army and had participated in the Soviet/Afghan war. After illegally finding their way to the United States, they had found other Soviet immigrants and intimidated them into participating in their criminal enterprises. They now lived under assumed names and identities and enjoyed a lavish lifestyle.

Whenever possible, Ernie made sure he accompanied me everywhere. He was a likable guy and I admired his knowledge of endless subjects, but I was worried he would not have my back if I needed him. I had no idea what he reported to the SAIC and didn't care, because whenever I needed to do something questionable while working on this case, I gave Ernie the slip, which was easy because he had no street experience.

After weeks of surveillance and interviewing victims, witnesses, and looking into the business practices of "Overseas Enterprises," the business name that Federoff and Lukin operated under, I could find only a few criminal violations. Actually, Ernie's analytical skills were very helpful for this kind of investigation.

After several private meeting with the U.S. Attorney's Office, we couldn't find anyone willing to prosecute these crooks based on the evidence we presented. It's extremely frustrating to know who the crooks are, but you don't have enough evidence to make a lawful arrest and get prosecution.

I think privately, Ernie and I secretly began to admire each other's different skill sets. In fact one evening when we were sitting in our office discussing this case, Ernie hit on it.

The notorious Chicago gangster, Al Capone, who couldn't be brought down on any major criminal activity, finally ended up in prison at Alcatraz for tax evasion. The police and feds knew he was guilty of murder, extortion, racketeering, conspiracy, bribery and scores of other offenses, but could only prove tax evasion.

Ernie and I finally found a cooperative IRS Agent, which is not an easy thing to do. The IRS is so restricted and regulated, that getting information from it usually requires a court order. They are a one way street, accepting information about anybody, but not willing to share. The good thing from a criminal standpoint is when the IRS points a finger at you, you are guilty unless you can prove innocence. Believe me, like most Americans, I am no fan of the IRS or our crippling taxation laws.

After Ernie and I devoted another two weeks jointly looking into the finances of Federoff,

The Russians

Lukin and Overseas Enterprises, we found we could not get excited. The IRS source uncovered several discrepancies that could justify an audit, at most would yield a fine and penalty and would not justify a lengthy prison sentence. We were disappointed and back to square one. Weeks of investigation had yielded nothing we could take to a Federal Grand Jury.

When I was in Tucson, I developed several strong relationships and worked closely with the U.S. Border Patrol, ICE (Immigration and Customs Enforcement). Tucson is only about 85 miles from the Mexico border and much of the criminal activity in the S.W. United States originates at the Arizona/Mexico border. Good liaison and relationships with ICE and Border Patrol Agents is essential if you are going to be effective at your job. Most criminal cases involve responsibilities that overlap into the enforcement activities of multiple agencies, federal, state, and local.

One day I received a call from Rudy Valdez, an ICE Agent in Tucson, regarding a case that we had worked on jointly 6 months prior. The case was now going to trial and the offenders were being extradited to Guatemala. Suddenly it hit me. Why hadn't I thought of this before? I began to share my case with Rudy. He agreed to look into the matter.

If we could not get Federoff, Lukin and some of their colleagues behind bars in the U.S. we would deport the bastards back to Russia where they came from. That would be a lot more painful than a cushy federal prison. Their assets could be seized and the Russian government would deal with them harshly as they are not happy when Russian citizens leave their country illegally.

Five days later Rudy called and verified that Federoff, Lukin and five other names we had provided were in the U.S. illegally and were using fictitious identities and social security numbers. That was it. That was more than enough to charge and extradite. Now we had to arrest them.

Ernie and I knew their properties, their residences, businesses and eating places. We had eavesdropped on their phone conversations and had piles of surveillance photographs. Some of these photos even contained Federoff with some California politicians and the Los Angeles District Attorney. No Surprise.

Ernie and I brought this matter to the attention of our squad leader and ASAIC. Up to now, I had received a lot of heat and criticism for wasting so much time and resources on this investigation. But, thanks to Ernie's input and backing, the supervisors approved the take down and offered up the manpower and resources necessary.

We know the only thing these Russians would respect was overwhelming force. We wanted surrender, not a gun fight. I decided on "Shock and Awe" borrowed from the Gulf War, where we hit the Iraqi soldiers with so much force so quickly, the war was over before it got going.

I spent the next few days assembling my arrest team and coordinating with my ICE counterpart in L.A. recommended by Rudy Valdez. His name was Rodney Hernandez, a big Mexican American in his early 40's who was an experienced field supervisor, well respected and above corruption. He was a "get it done" kind of guy (not a rule book, agency manual guy). Rodney also had an ugly scar that extended the length of his left jaw line.

Like I've said, I like guys with scars. Everybody called him "the Rod" or Rod to his face. I never knew why, but suspected it had something to do with the extendable baton he always carried openly on his belt. A 6" piece of steel that instantly telescopes into an 18" deadly weapon with the flick of the wrist. Agents refer to it as a rod. Secret Service Agents are issued a "rod" and receive extensive training on how to effectively use it, however many stop carrying their "rod" after a while because of its weight. I suspected that Rodney has some stories to tell, but I never asked.

When it comes to planning a raid or high profile arrest, the Secret Service lets the agent assigned the case call the shots and determine the manpower and equipment needed. The exception would be if the agent was an inexperienced rookie. Since I had more field experience than anybody in the squad, I didn't have anybody second guessing my requests. Obviously my main concern was safety.

Rodney and I were conflicted about where to conduct the arrests. We wanted to grab not only Federoff and Lukin, but as many of their Russian accomplices as possible before they vanished like cockroaches exposed to sunlight. The safest place as far as not endangering outsiders was the self storage facility in the valley. But the Russians didn't go there in mass. We would get a search warrant for that later.

I liked Federoff's residence on the bluff above the beach in Malibu, because there was no place to run. However, the entrance was protected by a heavy steel gate and we knew Federoff had 4

The Russians

American born children and a wife that lived there. I even considered the procedure I used with Orlando in Arizona, but concluded that wouldn't work with the Russians. So Rodney and I agreed the San Pedro dock and warehouse would be the best place. But when?

After monitoring telephone wire taps (the most boring thing in the world) for days, we finally got a break. The Russians always spoke English in their day to day affairs, but when talking about criminal activity, spoke Russian.

With the help of a translator loaned to us from the State Department, we became aware of a meeting that was going to occur at the San Pedro warehouse that upcoming Sunday at 11 p.m. We also knew that several foreign registered cargo/container ships would arrive in port that weekend. We were sure their gathering coincided with the arrival of one of the containers on one of the ships.

We had three days to prepare. We obtained surveillance photographs from the air. Fortunately at midnight on Sunday, there is only one entrance available to the San Pedro dock and it is monitored by private security. This meant we would need to smuggle most of our manpower and equipment in during day time business hours and they would need to stay hidden until midnight.

Rodney agreed to provide 10 of his top hand-picked ICE agents and I would provide 12 plus Ernie and I. I held the briefing Friday afternoon at the field office and gave out assignments. We invited LAPD and Harbor Patrol as a courtesy to attend a preliminary briefing without a lot of details because we didn't know who we could trust and didn't want any leaks.

As you can imagine there were a lot of unhappy moans and groans in the briefing room when the agents were informed they were giving up their Sunday for the cause. I don't know about ICE agents, but Secret Service Agents are expected to work anywhere, anytime, for as long as necessary for their meager salary. However, I think down deep any real field agent loves the adrenaline and danger of being involved in a case like this; especially if they don't have to do the paper work. Plus, they have something to tell their grandchildren someday.

At 9 p.m. Sunday everybody was in place. Snipers were on roof tops and positioned on lift cranes. ICE and Secret Service Agents were in various unlocked shipping containers on the docks. Radio traffic was encrypted. Overseas

The Russians

Enterprises was locked down. Even the SAIC was sitting in a surveillance van a safe distance away, observing the situation. Now the hardest part—waiting.

Finally! At 10:35 p.m. a white panel van without windows approached the San Pedro dock entrance gate. Two males occupied the front seat, but our pole cameras didn't allow us a clear enough picture to make identification. After entering the gate the van proceeded to the front of Overseas Enterprises. The passenger got out, unlocked the pedestrian door and went inside. In a few moments the rollup door opened. The van drove in and the door was closed. Ten minutes later two more matching white vans showed up and the process was repeated. The muscle had arrived.

My biggest concern was that the gray, cold marine layer that occupies the California coastline this time of year would not thicken. It was already starting to roll in and I was counting heavily on the snipers for protection as well as the "Shock and Awe" impact.

At exactly 11:25 p.m. a black Lincoln and a black Suburban pulled up to the gate. We knew the Lincoln would be carrying Federoff and Lukin. We weren't sure who was in the Suburban, but assumed it contained Russian criminals.

I had to constantly remind myself that the only charges we could enforce were immigration violations, unless they resisted arrest or we found contraband during our search incident to arrest. Of course there would also be illegal weapons violations that could be added. I waited for the black vehicles to pull up to the entrance of the roll up door. I requested radio silence.

As I stood there in the dark waiting, I quickly thought back to a childhood memory that had sustained me through my career in unpleasant assignments. I was 12 years old and our family pet had acquired rabies. He was just a mutt, but we loved that dog. My Dad told me to take the dog into a nearby field and shoot it. I objected but my Dad said, "Sometimes a man's got to do what needs to be done." Reluctantly, I carried out his order. Over the years those words of my father have sustained me and given me the courage to do what needs to be done.

The pedestrian door of the building opened and two Russians carrying automatic weapons stepped out and approached the vehicles. The windows came down and there were some exchanges in Russian. Not knowing what was said or what was going to happen next, I was unde-

The Russians

cided as to how to respond. Do I allow them to enter and the seal off the building? That could turn into a lengthy standoff or do we take them in the open. Rod whispered in my ear, "Remember what we are here for."

I gave the radio command— "NOW NOW NOW." Suddenly the nearby container door burst open and agents began to converge on the vehicles and building. I screamed into the load speaker, "THIS IS THE POLICE. DO NOT MOVE!"

The Russians were stunned, but one of the Russians with the automatic weapon raised his weapon and pointed it at an agent. Our sniper shot both of the Russians. That was going to require some creative report writing on my end. I ordered the occupants to exit the vehicle, but they didn't move; so I commanded the sniper to shoot out the tires and put a few rounds into the engine.

After what seemed like 5 minutes, but was only a few seconds the firing ceased. The back window of the Lincoln was lowered and a white cloth was tossed out. I then ordered Federoff to tell his men inside to come out. They cannot escape. After we had everyone outside and on the ground, we searched the building, but found no counterfeit or contraband. Hard to believe. Rod and I secured the building and posted a couple people there all night. We would return in the day light and conduct a more thorough search. It was going to be a long night.

Both of the shot up Russians survived, but lived very limited lives. We found no illegal contraband in the vehicles or the building, which to this day I feel we missed something. Federoff and Lukin at first thought the immigration charges were a joke until they along with six of their colleagues found themselves on a transport plane headed to Moscow. Even though we never found the counterfeit, its distribution in Southern California ceased after the arrests.

After that it became obvious to the other agents in my squad as well as the SAIC that I was a highly experienced agent and a leader who could oversee a major case.

Ernie was reassigned to other duties in the office. But we maintained a mutual respect for each other.

My fellow agents now thought I was OK. In fact I was soon invited out to lunch and for an off duty drink by other members of my squad. It was actually refreshing to be a working field agent again instead of a supervisor. I was now only responsible for myself and my teammates.

I only had to work my case load and did not have to spend most of my time sitting at a desk or meeting with other law-enforcement supervisors, bullshitting for hours.

I was once again actually doing the part of the job I enjoyed most. I became a "ghost" again around the office. As long as I produced the results, solved the cases I was assigned and arrested the bad guys, I was good.

Six months later the SAIC called me into his office for a closed door session. I was concerned. After asking about my wife and kids (like he cared) he said, "I don't know what happened to you in Arizona, but I'm very pleased with you and glad to have you in L.A. He then asked if I would be interested in taking over the Training and Fitness Division in the Los Angeles Field Office, where I could get out of the field case work and take it easy. I declined.

I was bitter about being in L.A. It was a terrible hardship on my family. I would not be able to come home to my family for weeks at a time. Needless to say, I hated my living conditions. I loved and missed my family. The job was hard enough on family life without this kind of arrangement added.

I had already missed so many of the things families do together. I had been absent for most of my own anniversaries and many family holidays. I had missed my daughter's dance recitals, drama plays, even her first words and steps learning to walk. I was absent for my son's soccer games, basketball and football games. His track meets. I loved my wife and kids and this separation was unbearable.

The Secret Service like most government agencies doesn't care about your family. Your personal life is not part of the equation. In fact many agents don't have a personal life. The job is their life and they give everything to it. The job becomes who they are. Very few agents who start out married finish their career that way or with children that still respect and admire them.

I did not want to finish that way. I made it a discipline to talk to my wife and children every day.

I blamed SAIC Spangler and ASAIC Baronowski. I was angry. I was bitter. My hatred of them grew with each passing day. I would make them pay. Those two pot bellied desk jockeys

The Russians

had no idea what I was capable of doing.

Every time I drove from L.A. to Tucson via Phoenix, I thought about how I would deliver payback. One way or another, I was going to make sure they did not live happily ever after.

A Double Minded Man

-30-

PAYBACK

It was December 28 6:37 AM. The Sonoran Desert is cold in Scottsdale, Arizona when the sun is not up. The temperature that night had dropped to 40°, but I didn't feel it. I was warm with the fire of revenge burning inside of me.

For the past 75 minutes, I had positioned myself against a pile of sandstone rubble, beside a huge three armed saguaro cactus, observing a family of Javelins munching their way across the desert floor about 20 yards away.

How an animal like that can walk up to a prickly pear cactus and start munching away on plants that are covered with spikes and stickers is beyond me. I also never bought into the claims by wild life experts, who say that Javelins are actually rodents. If something looks like a wild pig, acts like a wild pig, smells like a pig, it probably is a pig. Shouldn't take a college degree to figure that out.

But, I was not there to observe wildlife or watch another beautiful Sonoran Desert sunrise. It was payback time. Time to rid the world of that scumbag Spangler. I hated that bastard. I had never hated anyone like that before. Spangler should have been transferred from Arizona, not me.

I played it over and over in my mind a thousand times. Eleven months earlier SAIC Spangler had submitted a request that I be fired. His trumped up charges and accusations included falsifying government documents, unauthorized use of a government vehicle, sexual harassment, discrimination and neglect of duty.

All lies, lies, lies. All fabricated to have me removed because he was two years away from his pension and believed, in his alcoholic brain, that I wanted his job.

I had just driven approximately 300 miles in the dark of night from Los Angeles. But I was not tired. I was exhilarated. I had carefully planned this moment and now it was almost time. I was anxious. This was no random heat of passion slaying. This would be a 1st degree murder.

This was going to be the culmination of a well-planned execution of somebody who needed to be removed. Somebody who had ruined my life, my career and was hurting my family. I did not deserve this. But he was going to get what he deserved.

I had thought about this for months. I had carefully visited this location twice before. I had picked out the perfect spot and had visualized every aspect of this moment. Nothing could go wrong. There would be no evidence left behind, only Spangler's dead body for investigators to ponder.

I had concluded that Spangler liked to sit in his hot tub in the morning and clear his alcohol impaired brain cells. On my two prior visits, I had carefully watched his movements from the back door of his million dollar estate situated in the foothills of Northeast Scottsdale. I watched him walk across the cool decking of his patio, go to the South end of his swimming pool, disrobe and step into his hot tub. This was his morning ritual.

Spangler would never know what hit him. There would be little or no sound from the muzzle of the rifle. The special made 7 mm round would begin to fracture on impact with his head, leaving nothing for the investigators to analyze. Through the lens of the high-powered scope, I would see Spangler's head explode and his brains would be splattered all over the side of his beautiful 5,000 square-foot Santa Fe style desert home.

At 310 yards, I couldn't miss. The conditions were perfect. It was far better than he deserved.

At first I had planned to kidnap and torture the bastard to death over an extended period of time. I wanted to prolong his suffering as long as possible. Hear him beg for mercy. I wanted him to pay for what he had done to me and my family.

Even I didn't know what I was capable of. The government had trained me well.

After that, I would eventually "off" that little son of a bitch ASAIC Baronowski, Spangler's little ass kissing, go to man. Baronowski was the brains of the Phoenix field office, who at Spangler's request had fabricated and compiled the bogus charges against me.

Baronowski was going to pay also. I can hear his pathetic words echoing in my ears now "Nothing personal Glenn, just following orders." All the time pretending we are brothers in arms, but behind my back trying to build a case against me.

Well this is just business for me also. Personal business, and when it is finished then I can get on with my life. Or so I had convinced myself.

I believe people are by nature bad but capable of doing much good. Many believe the opposite. At that point in my life most of my time was consumed by bad people. You tend to become like the people with whom you associate.

I believe if you squeeze people hard enough it will surprise you what comes out. Most of us are posers. Pretending to be something we really aren't and put on a good front for those we know.

I must have been thinking of other things. Suddenly I realized that Spangler was already outside and was walking across the cool decking. It caught me by surprise. But, no problem, my plan was to wait until he was sitting calmly in the hot tub, stationary. There I would have a perfect view of his head from the shoulders up.

As I began to settle the crosshairs on to his head, and adjust for distance and elevation, I detected movement. It was his trophy wife and

11-year-old daughter. They came out the door and were crossing the decking toward Spangler.

Oh No! God! This wasn't supposed to happen. This is not how I planned this scene. Can't anything go right?

They were talking to him, removing their bathrobes and entering the hot tub.

My mind was racing, should I go ahead and blow his brains out in front of his wife and daughter? Why not? But they were not to blame for his misdeeds. Instantly I thought of my own wife and daughter. I thought about the image an act like this would leave on their minds. Dammit! I couldn't do this. I slowly moved my right index finger away from the trigger of the rifle. I continued to stare at Spangler and his family through the rifle scope for another minute or two.

Suddenly I was overwhelmed with emotion. I thought about how much I loved my own wife and children. Tears began to well up in my eyes. It was a strange sensation. I had not experienced tears in a long time. I had forced myself to become desensitized and emotionless. I felt an overwhelming sense of guilt. What was I doing? How would this act help my situation or my family?

Payback

I slowly wiped the tears off of my cheeks with my rough knit glove and carefully made my way through the rugged terrain and cacti back to my vehicle, which was parked about 200 yards away.

After securing my rifle and brushing myself off, I sat in my vehicle and stared at the beautiful sunrise. The vibrant colors were spectacular. For a moment I thought I was staring at the face of God and again began to weep. I asked God for forgiveness.

This was definitely not the outcome I had planned and prepared so carefully for the past few months. But somehow I knew it was the right thing. Suddenly it seemed as though a huge weight had been lifted off my back.

There are moments in life that bring clarity. This was one of those. Without knowing it, I had been at a crossroads and a short movement of my finger on hard metal stood poised to define the state of my soul. What had I been prepared to do—to mete out justice as I saw it? A force much greater than myself had intervened, giving me enough time to see that my actions would have taken me down a much darker road, one with no return. And that other road? It was the path of forgiveness—the same forgiveness that my God had shown when he died for me. I was humbled and transformed as I walked away…and I was free.

So this is what forgiveness feels like.

Payback

A Double Minded Man

-31-

EXITING

It was time to think about an exit strategy. I was getting old and over the hill by Secret Service agent standards.

I still had a beautiful, faithful wife who had put up with all the Secret Service bullshit - all the assignment, the moves, transfers, promotions, demotions and reassignments.

She had raised our two wonderful children who are now teenagers. Children who still loved and respected me but didn't know who their father really was.

With the exception of the occasional bad dreams, I was a normal husband, father and member of society who even went to church and worshiped on Sundays. The dreams were and still are the worst part. Sometimes I spend the whole night working in my mind. Sometimes it becomes violent. My poor wife has been punched and kicked more times then she can remember. I always feel terrible after I have unintentionally hurt her. We sleep in a king size bed so she can keep her distance when she needs to.

I began to think about being in business for myself. I wanted to be my own boss. Never take an order again. Get paid based on my performance versus what a position is worth. I was tired of the ass kissing and politicking that it takes to get ahead in government. I was determined to never again be evaluated annually, by somebody in Washington, D.C., who didn't even know who I am.

My physical injuries had been extensive over my 18 year career: three knee surgeries, my neck vertebrae's were fused together leaving me with limited range of motion. My right wrist had been crushed and several bones had been removed. Surgery had pieced it back together leaving it with very little movement. Bone had been removed from both sides of my pelvis to repair my neck and wrist.

So, I was no longer young and strong and fearless at 45 like I was at 31. Things now hurt all the time and I'm sure my reflexes aren't as sharp.

Like I said, it's a young guy's job. Even better if you're single because then you can work and travel all the time, since you have nothing to come home to.

For the past two years in my spare time I had been studying and looking at different businesses to start. I had stayed up late watching various infomercials. I had scoured through dozens of entrepreneurial magazines. I looked at numerous franchise opportunities and home-based businesses. The last thing I wanted to do was go find another job and have somebody else telling me what time I had to be at work, when to eat lunch, what time to go home and when I could have time off for a personal life. I was done taking orders, asking permission and allowing other people to tell me what I was worth.

It should be obvious, but I don't think most people understand the simple principle that you become who you associate with. We also take advice from people who are unqualified to give advice on that subject. We end up asking friends, relatives, coworkers or people we associate with what they think about this or that, when they aren't qualified to give advice on the matter. My friend, Bill Hawkins always says "Opinions are like armpits. Everybody has a couple and they usually stink."

One day a friend of my wife's introduced us to a successful doctor by the name of Mike Scott. During the course of our brief conversation he asked something that impacted the rest of my life. He asked "What are your dreams?" At 26 when I was in law school I could've answered that. At 31, I still could have answered that. But now, in my early 40s I didn't have an answer. The more I pondered the question the realization came to me that I no longer had any dreams. It was one of the saddest moments of my life.

I remember leaving that meeting with Dr. Mike Scott, sitting in my car and tearing up for the first time in years. The realization began to sink into my brain that I no longer had any real dreams. Things I wanted to accomplish, places I wanted to go. Opportunities and experiences I wanted to provide for my family. Nothing. All gone. Just going through life in survival mode living paycheck to paycheck.

How pathetic. Over time the grind of life takes away your dreams and turns you into a re-alist.

Exiting

After a few more conversations with Dr. Scott, he introduced me to an international business development organization that he was a part of called Worldwide Dream Builders (WWDB). It was an unknown entity made up of people from all walks of life and social economic levels. They were a coaching and mentoring organization who showed people how to take advantage of economic trends and create financial freedom.

I discovered that WWDB is a billion dollar LLC (limited liability company) that has partnered with Amway Corporation, one of the largest, privately owned, debt free companies in the world. Amway is short for American Way and manufactures over 450 consumer goods for home, health, beauty and personal care. Their products have been ranked #1 in online sales for years. Amway has over 19,000 employees and operate in 100 plus countries. They now hold almost 1200 patents and retain 900+ scientists in 75 laboratories .

WWDB partners with Amway to teach people to be independent business owners and create generational financial freedom.

WWDB emphasizes personal growth and development in all areas of one's life : spiritual, mental, physical, relational, marital, and leadership. Not just financial. They also teach people how to be debt free and live below their means.

Knowledge, ambition and motivation are useless, unless applied to something useful and meaningful. WWDB gives you the knowledge, skill, mentoring and an environment for success, but Amway gives you the vehicle to apply it to.

This was confirmation of what I had always believed: It's not what you know, it's who you know and are they willing to help you?

Dr. Scott soon introduced me to a man named Ross Hall. Ross Hall was unlike anyone I had ever met before. A tall thin man in his 50s, who had retired from his government job in his early 30s and was now a multimillionaire. He seemed to ooze peace, joy and confidence. He spoke philosophically and with metaphors. He lived on such a higher mental level than I did, that much of the time I did not know what he was talking about or understood what he was saying.

Ross Hall introduced me to his friend and mentor, Theron Nelsen. Theron was a laid back Idaho native, who had been raised on a farm. He was also the cofounder of WWDB and his coaching and mentoring had helped hundreds of people create financial freedom.

Exiting

Theron Nelsen was the antithesis of Ross Hall, even though they had been college fraternity brothers. Unlike Ross, who talked to me with glowing metaphors and spiritual truths, with wisdom beyond my understanding: Theron was full of down to earth, one sentence answers to the most complex questions. Theron is the most self assured, confident man I've ever met. A former NFL player for the Denver Broncos, and an ophthalmologist, Theron treats everyone with love and kindness.

Ross and Theron helped me realize that society had bought into the lie of: Go to school, get a good education, so you can go get a good job and work for somebody else the rest of your life. As long as I worked for someone else, I was building their dream, not mine.

Of course, I was skeptical at first. At that point in my life I was non trusting of everyone and skeptical and critical of everything. I had seen too many scams. Heard too many lies. Experienced too many disappointments and been let down by too many people. I truly hoped these people were for real.

However I did know how to investigate, track down people, obtain information and analyze evidence. So if these people in WWDB weren't for real, I would find out and expose them.

Top secret government clearance allows you to gain access to just about anything you want. If you make something into a federal case with an assigned case number, then you can really get information about people, organizations and companies.

After a two month investigation, I had acquired information and reviewed data provided by the Better Business Bureau, Dunn and Bradstreet, Justice Department, Treasury Department, Department of Labor, Department of Commerce, Fortune and Success Magazine, UCC Files, Federal Trade Commission, Dow Theory Files, State Attorney General's Office and financial records on several WWDB members, who would later impact my life. I had all the evidence I needed to trust WWDB and submit to their leadership and mentorship.

I was amazed at what I found. In fact, it looked too good to be true. Here was an organization of men and women who would invest the most precious thing they have (their time and resources) into me and my family to help us achieve our dreams and goals.

There had to be a catch. Maybe this was a

Exiting

cult. Yet, I had utilized every resource I knew. Had looked under every rock I could find. Everything seemed legit. I just needed to convince Mike Scott, Ross Hall and Theron Nelsen that my family would be a good investment for them.

Eventually, I was able to meet and spend time with the current leader of WWDB, Ron Puryear. The most humble, multimillionaire, I've ever known.

A handshake between Ron Puryear and Theron Nelsen, 42 years ago had turned into a billion dollar LLC, with 15 different divisions that has improved the lives of countless people around the world.

Success in all areas of your life seems to boil down to two things: Are you willing to be coached and mentored by people who have the kind of life you desire? And, you become like the people you associate with. Associate with people who have the life you want.

People should stop taking advice from people who have no fruit on their trees.

I also met men and women I could respect and admire. People whose lives, marriages, morals and character represented excellence. People who came from every conceivable background and occupation, who now have the number one lifestyle in America but use their time and resources to serve and mentor others. People who could do or have anything they want. Men like Howie Danzik, former physical therapist. Bob Kummer, former corporate manager and Olympic runner. Jimmy Head, former rock-n-roller and founder of the Del Rays surf band. Bill Hawkins, English teacher and genius. Norm Kizirian, successful medical business man.

I also met some real warriors, like Lynn Burnett an Army Ranger, Frank Radford a Navy Seal and Mike Carrol a Navy Seal, plus countless others, whose lives and lifestyles represented everything I wanted for my family but didn't know was possible. People who created financial freedom in their 20's and 30's. People I could respect and desired to be respected by.

Everything in my life began to change as a result of the influence and association I received from the successful people in WWDB. I was even able to develop a close friendship with WWDB's spiritual advisor and counselor Paul Tsika and his wife Billy Kay, who opened up a whole new dimension of my life. Their counseling helped to heal the fractured relationships in our family, between my children and I. They showed me how

Exiting

to live to please God, not man.

WWDB helped us start and create a successful home-based business we called Legacy Marketing. Within three years we were out of debt, earning more money in our part time business than I was earning after 19 years in the Secret Service.

I was 45 years old, but I now had options I never had before. I had dreams again.

I remember leaving Tucson one Sunday afternoon and driving west on my return trip to Los Angeles, after a brief 20 hour visit with my family. I hated that 400+ mile drive back to Los Angeles into the blazing blindness of the setting sun.

When I walked into my office, in the middle of the desk, there it was. The final nail in the coffin. That extra ounce that would create the tipping point. It was a piece of paper telling me that I was to report to Washington, D.C. for briefing and training. I was going to be leading an advance team that would leap frog ahead of President Bill Clinton making security preparations for his presidential reelection campaign. This would mean approximately nine months of living out of a suitcase and traveling all over the country.

After calling Ross Hall and evaluating my financials I made a life-changing decision. I was done.

I had heard many testimonials from other members of WWDB about their elaborate retirement parties with hundreds of their friends and business associates in attendance. I had imagined and pictured something like that in my mind for me someday. But that was not to be. I was going to go out the same way I came in, with no fanfare, but it didn't matter.

I calmly walked to the supply office and retrieved a couple of cardboard boxes. Slowly, I began to remove pictures from my wall and personal effects from my desk. After I had boxed and sealed everything I cared about, I walked into the SAIC's office and closed the door behind me. I then put the advance team orders on his desk and said, "Find someone else I'm not going. In fact I'm leaving and going home effective now." He was stunned at first and didn't know what to say.

I explained, "I'm done. I'm done with the Secret Service and I'm going home."

Exiting

He pointed out, "If you leave now you will not receive any retirement." I explained that I had accumulated months of unused leave and effective now I was going on vacation. After vacation, I would be on leave without pay for the duration of the next year until my 20 year career was complete. I assured him that I already checked with legal affairs in Washington and that the only consequence would be a reduced pension when the time came.

I packed up all of my official government gear, cleaned out my car and returned to the SAIC's office.

He informed me that he had called legal affairs and confirmed that everything I said was accurate. He then complimented me on my contribution to the Secret Service and acknowledged that I had received a raw deal and was sorry to see me go.

I then removed my weapon, unloaded it and placed it on his desk. I told him I would keep my commission book until 20 years was completed and then would mail it back to the office.

We then shook hands and I walked out.

By then my squad members had got wind of

what I was doing and insisted on taking me to lunch and having a few drinks even though it was only 10 a.m.

Before leaving the Los Angeles field office for the last time, I called my wife and told her it was over, that I was free and coming home.

I drove the next 400 miles back to Tucson in silence, replaying the past 19 years of my life in my brain.

I was 45 years old.
I had served 5 presidential administrations.
I was finally free.
Or was I?

Exiting

A Double Minded Man

-32-

NSS AGAIN

If you were over 10 years old in 2001, you remember.

It's embedded in your mind forever.

On September 11, 2001, I was sitting at the Southwest terminal at Tucson International Airport waiting to board a flight to Sacramento, California. It was strangely quiet in the terminal. There was no jet noise. The power had been shut down on all of the television sets that are usually on. People were milling about, but they were silent. Soon an announcement came over the PA system, that all flights had been canceled.

As I got in my car and began to drive home I turned to the radio. Like the rest of the world, I eventually learned that 19 Muslim fanatic, brain washed cowards had hijacked and used American airliners to kill 3000 innocent civilians without regard for anyone.

Suddenly, all of America was shaken from its slumber and apathy. We were reminded once again that the world is a dangerous place and America has enemies who do not want to convert or change your point of view, they want you and everything about you DEAD, DEAD, DEAD.

Within days, the phone began to ring. They had found me. I said no! I thought about the pressure my former agent colleagues must be under. I'm sure all leave and days off had been canceled. Still I said no. I had put all of that behind me and was enjoying my new life, my family and growing my business. Besides, it now seems like somebody else had lived my previous life. I now had new association. New friends. I surrounded myself with positive people. I had read dozens of positive mental attitude and self help books. I didn't think the same as before and I was no longer the same man. In fact I never even talk to anybody about my past.

I even changed my phone number, but within a few days my phone rang again. How did they find me? I knew the answer to that. You can always be found. Every time I saw an incoming

274

phone call with a Washington, D.C. area code, I ignored it and told my family to do the same. So they tried a new strategy.

One morning I answered a phone call from an area code I did not recognize. On the other end was a voice I hadn't heard in years. A voice that brought back memories I had long since suppressed. Memories about someone I had buried, but now seems to be rising from the grave and clawing his way to the surface like some kind of horror movie.

It was Burton Vance.

Again I said no!

Soon I was hearing a speech about duty and honor and country and sacrifice. A speech about freedom and America and Americans doing what needed to be done. A speech very similar to one I had heard many years ago in a Roy Rogers restaurant in downtown Washington, D.C.

Sure I was outraged by the atrocities of 9/11/2001 but I wasn't a young warrior anymore.

Vance was very persuasive. He knew I loved what America stands for: Freedom, Opportunity, Free Enterprise, Capitalism, Family. The things that make our country great for everyone.

He also knew I despised politics and most politicians and that politics would never permit the things that needed to be done.

Intelligence needed to be gathered now. Enemies of America had to be destroyed.

I agreed to a limited response. The targets had to be valid and positively identified.

I then submitted a list of items I required. Four days later a plain white van arrived at my front door and after providing identification and a signature, everything I had requested was sitting at my front door. Fortunately no one else was home. How did they know where I lived? They know everything.

Over the next few years the dialogue between Vance and I consisted of:
"It's done."
"Any collateral damage?"
"No"
"Any loose ends?"
"No"
"Good. And good day."

NSS Again

A Double Minded Man

-33-

ONLY THE BEST

To be perfectly clear, I believe the U.S. Secret Service is one of, if not the finest federal law enforcement agency in the United States. They are the first and oldest, established in 1865.

The agent qualification standards are extremely challenging, only the best, about one out of every 300 qualified applicants make it through the actual hiring process. I hope those high standards are never lowered.

The agency has had its share of bad publicity in recent years, but I believe that is a top down issue. It is a reflection of president appointed leadership of people who aren't qualified to lead an agency like the USSS. Traditionally, the top leadership in the Secret Service have worked their way up thru the ranks to the top and earned their stripes. Therefore, they have the respect of the rank and file agents who they are known by. But when you have the Executive Branch of Government appointing unqualified people to these positions based on race and gender, then morale is low and performance suffers.

The demands and responsibilities placed upon Secret Service agents are daunting. They must provide safety and security for the President, Vice President and their families, as well as for every foreign leader that comes to the United States or its territories. They also protect the candidates who run for election every four years. At the same time they must defend the nation's financial and cyber institutions from fraud, corruption and counterfeit. Their duties must be carried out without error or delay.

The job is definitely not for everyone, but for those few who qualify, they will go places and have experiences that others can only imagine.

I have nothing but respect for the men and women serving today. I am honored to have served and proud to have been an agent of the United States Secret Service.

Only The Best

A Double Minded Man

CONCLUSION

I often wonder if anything I did mattered. Did it really make a difference?

A contractor can point to a building he has constructed.

A composer, to a song they have created.

A writer, to a book they've written.

An artist, to a painting they have created.

But a Secret Service agent has nothing tangible to show for their time, effort or sacrifice.

How does one know what they contributed?

What they prevented?

How do they know if anything in the past, present or future is any different because they served?

GOD ONLY KNOWS . . .

A Double Minded Man

AUTHOR'S NOTE

It had always been my original intention to take these memories and experiences to the grave. There are many other things I could share, but have chosen not to mentally relive them at this time.

After many years of requests from family and friends, I have chosen to share these few stories.

Now you know.

Glenn

A Double Minded Man

DISCLAIMER

Most of the stories presented in this book have some merit. Some of the stories may actually be true. However, I believe it best to proceed as if not a single word in this book relates to any actual place or person in the past, or present real world. Consider it to be a work of fiction.

Made in the USA
Middletown, DE
08 October 2018